THE
GOVERNMENT LEADER'S
FIELD GUIDE TO
ORGANIZATIONAL
AGILITY

THE
GOVERNMENT LEADER'S
FIELD GUIDE TO
ORGANIZATIONAL
AGILITY

How to Navigate Complex and Turbulent Times

Sarah C. Miller

Shelley A. Kirkpatrick, PhD

Berrett–Koehler Publishers, Inc.

Berrett-Koehler Publishers, Inc.
1333 Broadway, Suite 1000
Oakland, CA 94612-1921
Tel: (510) 817-2277   Fax: (510) 817-2278   www.bkconnection.com

Ordering information

Quantity sales. Special discounts are available on quantity purchases by corporations, associations, and others. For details, contact the "Special Sales Department" at the Berrett-Koehler address above.

Individual sales. Berrett-Koehler publications are available through most bookstores. They can also be ordered directly from Berrett-Koehler:
Tel: (800) 929-2929; Fax: (802) 864-7626; www.bkconnection.com.

Orders for college textbook / course adoption use. Please contact Berrett-Koehler: Tel: (800) 929-2929; Fax: (802) 864-7626.

Distributed to the U.S. trade and internationally by Penguin Random House Publisher Services.

Berrett-Koehler and the BK logo are registered trademarks of Berrett-Koehler Publishers, Inc.

Printed in the United States of America

Berrett-Koehler books are printed on long-lasting acid-free paper. When it is available, we choose paper that has been manufactured by environmentally responsible processes. These may include using trees grown in sustainable forests, incorporating recycled paper, minimizing chlorine in bleaching, or recycling the energy produced at the paper mill.

CIP data for this book is available at the Library of Congress.

ISBN: 978-1-5230-9341-0

First Edition

27   26   25   24   23   22   21   10   9   8   7   6   5   4   3   2   1

Book producer: Westchester Publishing Services
Cover designer: Peggy Archambault

To my parents, Susan and Richard
—Sarah C. Miller

Contents

Tools

Preface

Whew, 2020 was quite a year to write a book on organizational agility! If 2020 didn't make the case that we are all dealing with constant change, much of which we can't anticipate, then we don't know what does. We started writing in January of 2020, working side by side at a whiteboard as we developed the outline. That way of working soon changed, as it did for almost everyone, and we transitioned to virtual meetings for our collaboration. Not only did we have to adapt how we wrote together, but the world also became even more uncertain and complex as we navigated rapidly evolving health advice, interacted with friends and family in new ways, and observed tremendous social change. We know that government organizations at all levels—federal, state, and local—have faced just as much change and complexity. If you are a leader in a government organization—and by that, we mean both those in positions of formal authority as well as those who show leadership through their actions—we hope that this book provides guidance on how to manage work differently than you did in the past to meet the ever-changing challenges of the present. We've focused our advice on how you can organize your work in the midst of today's swirl of change.

The book offers a roadmap for how to lead. We encourage you to use it as a guide rather than a checklist or a formula. You might start by reading it from front to back, but we want you to continue to use it as a hands-on resource that you can refer back to as you help your organization navigate change. We've worked hard to go beyond platitudes ("be flexible," "just adapt") by describing actions that you can take and providing tools to get you started. While we've tried to be specific with our advice, we also realize that every situation is different, so we urge you to apply our counsel in a way that makes sense for the work that you do.

Another way that we bring our ideas to life is through Blair's story. We chose to frame this hypothetical story around an acquisition group because that's a common function across federal, state, and local government. That said, we believe that our story and the challenges that Blair and her team face will resonate with you no matter what type of work you do. And, although the story focuses on Blair, who is in a supervisory role, we recognize that agility is a journey that everyone in the organization takes. While some actions require support from someone in a position of authority, becoming more agile requires everyone, including individual contributors, to play a role. You will be able to implement almost all the concepts that we cover, whether you are an executive-level leader, mid-level leader, first-line supervisor, or individual contributor. The specific work that is done varies with each role; for example, executive-level leaders have responsibility for strategic planning activities, while first-line supervisors are more tactically focused. And each role may have to deal with both unique and common environmental factors; for example, dealing with pressure from Congress may be a highly salient challenge to an executive-level leader, while integrating new technologies into work processes may pose difficulties that supervisors and individual contributors must address. Regardless of one's role, each type of leader will need to apply the levers, starting with their immediate team, if they are to improve agility.

The book focuses specifically on government organizations, partly because we are familiar with the unique challenges those organizations face and partly because we realized that few books are aimed specifically at government leaders, especially those books on organizational agility. Many books and articles provide advice for addressing organizational agility in for-profit organizations, and while there are similarities between for-profit and not-for-profit organizations, certain concepts (e.g., competitive factors, revenues, and profits) simply don't apply to those in the not-for-profit sector.

The advice that we provide is evidence-based. The appendix contains an overview of the organizational agility model that we developed specifically for government organizations, along with select research that we relied on when building this model. Although we don't want to bore you with references supporting every idea in our book, we do want to assure you that our ideas are based on sound research and accepted practice. Many of the ideas we present here may not seem new to you. What is new, however, is how these time-tested ideas can support agility. While little change will likely result from trying only one or two of these ideas, we encourage you to start somewhere and act on as many of the ideas as you can. We anticipate you will start to see the benefits of agility as you and your team begin to experiment with and iterate how you approach and organize your work.

THE
GOVERNMENT LEADER'S
FIELD GUIDE TO
ORGANIZATIONAL
AGILITY

Constant Change Requires a Different Way of Organizing

Let's start with a story about a leader named Blair, who realizes that her organization and team face many challenges. She knows that the changes will not go away. In fact, the number and pace of changes will only increase, resulting in more complex and unexpected changes to deal with. Blair is just starting to see the need to find a different way of approaching work.

Blair, a mid-level manager in the acquisition department of a large government agency, gets settled in her home office. Some days Blair works remotely to give her space for deep, focused work; other days she heads into the office for face-to-face meetings. To start her workday, she thinks about her plan for the day. She logs into email, checking to see which problems will likely consume her day and take her away from the project she's been trying to launch. A message from her boss, Ms. Barton, catches her eye—it's a memo to their department of about a thousand employees. Ms. Barton has just attended a virtual contracting conference and has decided that the department needs to become "more agile" to meet increasing demand for the department's contracting services. Blair shakes her head, muttering, "Whatever that means!" Reading between the lines of the email, she starts to think about how this coming change will be just another way to squeeze more hours out of her and her staff. There certainly will be no increases to their budget, and her department is already understaffed, with several unfilled positions.

Still, she agrees with her boss; they do need to speed up the acquisitions process, because it's the only way to meet the demands of the program managers while also responding to constantly changing program needs. Being new to this job—she'd held a similar role in another agency until taking this position a month ago—Blair hasn't even settled into a routine yet. She'd heard that this department had challenges before she applied, but she's finding that the difficulties are more than just annoyances. They are obstacles to any kind of predictable productivity. In addition to the layers of regulations they have to legally adhere to in meeting-acquisition requests, her team is dealing with a lot of turbulence. The agency programs that they support have needs that are different from those in the past. The team's make-up is also changing, as team members now transfer from other parts of the agency instead of staying in acquisition for their entire career as they used to do. As a result, team members typically have less expertise in acquisition but also more understanding of the agency's mission. Team members are now working from home frequently too, so they might need new technologies to help them be more productive. She's even hearing about new acquisition tools coming soon that use artificial intelligence to draft contracts. But it's hard to stay on top of every new tool that's out there. And while it used to be a rare snowstorm that disrupted the team's work for a day or two, now it seems their work is disrupted for more reasons than ever—political factors, social unrest, pandemics. Add in all of the changes in the agency—new policies, changing regulations, major and minor restructurings, leaders coming and going—and it feels like a constant swirl of disruption.

And now, her boss wants her to make this dysfunctional organization "more agile"?!

Like Blair, you might find yourself saying that you just need to get ahead of the curve or that, if things would only slow down, your team would be able to reach its potential. Maybe you've found time to create a plan to examine how your team is approaching its work, only to find that the situation is more complex than you realized or that there's no time to put the plan into place because unforeseen events constantly pop up.

TOOL 1.1: How Does Your Team Experience Change?

Let's start with a quick check-in to see how complex and uncertain change generally affects your team. In the list of items below, place an *X* or checkmark along the line in the "Your Response" column to indicate how you and your team are experiencing change.

How Does Your Team Experience Change?

Item	Your Response
My team can't keep up with the pace of change.	Does not describe my situation — Completely describes my situation
My team often feels that we're behind the curve.	Does not describe my situation — Completely describes my situation
My team doesn't have enough time to plan its work.	Does not describe my situation — Completely describes my situation
Unexpected changes just keep coming.	Does not describe my situation — Completely describes my situation
When we do develop plans, they are quickly outdated when the situation changes.	Does not describe my situation — Completely describes my situation
The way we're approaching our work is not getting us the results we need.	Does not describe my situation — Completely describes my situation
Our workload keeps growing, yet we don't have more resources.	Does not describe my situation — Completely describes my situation

TOOL 1.1 (*continued*)

Item	Your Response	
The demands on my time never seem to end.	•——————————————• Does not describe my situation	Completely describes my situation
Despite all of the changes going on around us, my team is still expected to perform.	•——————————————• Does not describe my situation	Completely describes my situation
Simply working harder or more hours isn't enough to deal with all of the changes that affect my team.	•——————————————• Does not describe my situation	Completely describes my situation

If most of your checkmarks are toward the right side of the line, then you are experiencing an unending number of demands on your time, budget, and staff that are compounded by rapid and unexpected change. Even if you believe in your employees, your boss, and your colleagues, and you are committed to your organization's mission, you may not be getting the results that you want because the world around you keeps changing in ways that you don't expect.

Unfortunately, our world is not likely to slow down or become less complex. The changes that you are experiencing are not likely to become more straightforward or easier to understand. If anything, changes are likely to come at you faster, in an even less predictable way.

If you were leading an organization a hundred years ago, things might not have been so chaotic. As the Industrial Revolution changed trade into business in the eighteenth and nineteenth centuries, decisions were made at the top of the organization for a reason: it was efficient to centralize authority. Leaders acquired the information they needed to make good decisions, which they then communicated to those who were required to follow them. Employees could, with relative ease, be quickly taught to carry out their part in a process; if one person left, another could be quickly trained to replace that person. In a stable environment, leaders had time to gather information, make an effective decision, communicate it, and expect that it would be followed.

Today, traditional organizational principles, such as command-and-control, centralized decision-making, and siloed departments, don't always work well because the modern world's expectations of authority have changed. Instead, in today's constantly evolving environment, you need to find ways to help your colleagues and stakeholders adapt to changes while still being effective and efficient. That is, your organization needs to find a way to be more agile. We define *organizational agility* as being able to sense and respond to changes in both a timely and effective manner. Let's explore this definition a bit more.

Everyone in your organization—all employees, those in leadership roles as well as individual contributors—should know what is going on in the world around them that might affect their work. We call this *sensing*. You might be paying attention to changes outside the organization—new laws or policies, societal trends, advances in technology, customers with new needs, or even naturally occurring events such as a pandemic or natural disaster—as well as changes from within the organization—reorganizations, leadership changes, policy changes, and budget or resource changes.

Once you know what's going on around you, you can figure out what these changes mean to your mission and work. We call this *interpreting*. For example, you might read an article about a new software package and wonder if it could be used to do your work more efficiently; you could find another article to read, schedule a demo with the software company, and begin a conversation with your organization's technology experts as well as with senior staff whose work might be impacted.

After figuring out that changes in your environment could affect the organization in unpredictable ways, you need to figure

TOOL 1.1 (*continued*)

out what to do about it. We call this *responding*. You might decide to continue to keep an eye out to see if something that might change actually does. For example, you might attend a demonstration of the new software package and find out that it doesn't do exactly what you need right now but that the developer plans to add features in the next version. So you ask your technology experts to let you know when the new version comes out.

On the other hand, you might decide that a certain change really isn't something you need to worry about—it won't affect the organization in any material way, so you don't need to figure out how to respond. An example of this might be a new policy that updates certain regulations. You might read a memo that explains the update and learn that the change doesn't apply to your work. Or you might decide that the changes that you are sensing could disrupt the organization and your own work, so you need to start figuring out how you should respond—as individuals and as a team. For example, you might read an industry report that highlights a new trend of fewer college students majoring in your field; this might affect the organization's ability to recruit employees, and your human resource strategy might need to be updated to reflect this shift.

With so much in flux, everyone in the organization needs to begin the habits of sensing, interpreting, and responding. In other words, a constant focus on what's happening in the environment, along with figuring out what to do if a particular change materializes, needs to become routine. As such, we use the term *agility routines* to refer to ongoing sensing, interpreting, and responding actions that need to become second nature to everyone in the organization.

Being able to sense and respond quickly and effectively requires that leaders facilitate organizing the work in a way that can adjust to flux. Our definition of organizational agility uses the word *timely* because what is "quick enough" depends on the situation. Organizations must always be sure to respond effectively—that is, they must provide a response that is good. Responding quickly enough with the wrong response doesn't help anyone achieve the mission; responding too late with the right response also doesn't provide the outcomes you need. The response must be the right solution at the right time.

We've done the legwork to help you figure out how to position your organization for a turbulent environment: our knowledge of academic research combined with our own experience as organizational consultants enabled us to create an organizational agility framework. A framework is a way of presenting the elements in a system. Our framework contains the essential elements of an agile organization and provides a way to think about how your organization works and why. The Appendix provides the details of the framework, along with references should you choose to do additional research on your own.

When your organization aligns with the tempo and challenges in which you operate, you are more likely to achieve your mission, and your staff are more likely to be productive and engaged. People can do their jobs effectively and as quickly as necessary when the organization employs agility principles.

The organizational agility framework consists of three main parts: the changes going on in the world around you (which we call the *environment*), the organization (where the agility routines and levers come into play), and the outcomes achieved by the organization. This framework—and the research that it's based on—says that you are more likely to get the results that you want if you carry out work in a way that aligns with the changes and demands placed on your organization. When your world is changing quickly and in new and unpredictable ways, you must get everyone in the organization to play some role in the agility routine. To do that, you need to organize, or use the levers, in a way that supports the routines. Let's take a quick walk through the various parts of the framework.

MAKE SENSING AND INTERPRETING
ROUTINE BEHAVIORS

Sensing means noticing that something has changed, and *interpreting* refers to understanding what those changes mean for the organization. Not only are there more things to track than in the past, but all of those factors are also changing rapidly and probably in complex, ambiguous ways that make them hard to understand. The tools below provide different approaches to naming and exploring factors and trends so that you can start to identify the things that are affecting your organization or might affect it in the future.

To recognize what has happened, is currently happening, or is about to happen, you need to involve your employees in sensing. If they are not aware that something has happened, they can't respond to it. For example, when organizations fail to pick up on new customer requirements or aren't aware of new technologies that could help them work more efficiently, they are failing at sensing. Often, frontline employees have insight into these areas that those in management might not be as focused on.

In a traditional organization, sensing was usually done only by leaders, often in the form of updating an annual strategic plan; this approach worked well when things were more predictable. In an agile organization, however, everyone in the organization needs to sense what is going on around them. Of course, not everyone should be looking at the same things. People will naturally gravitate toward what they are interested in and perhaps to what they have expertise in. As a leader, you may want to learn more about what signals and information people are already paying attention to, so that you can identify any gaps and ask someone to look after those gaps. You might rely on your IT experts or engineers to sense new technologies or new ways to use existing technologies. Others may gravitate toward watching demographic trends that could impact your customer base or workforce. People in coordinator or liaison roles may already be aware of events happening elsewhere in the organization that could have implications for your work. Executives may talk to leaders in other organizations to find out what shifts and patterns they are concerned about. The point is that people at all levels of the organization should be able to get involved in some type of sensing.

As you start to gather all this information, you then need to interpret what it means for your organization. People often pick up on signals, data points, or other information that tells them something has changed, but they don't always know what that change means. The signals and data points might need to be combined with other information in order to fully understand what it means. People with a wide range of expertise might be needed to interpret the signals—people with technical or functional expertise; leaders who can help interpret what the signals mean for the organization's mission, strategy, or resources; staff members who have seen similar signals in other organizations; and long-tenured employees who have seen something similar in the past.

TOOL 1.2: Identify Factors That Influence Your Organization

The list of factors below will help you to identify influences on your organization. Factors include all of the events, trends, and patterns that impact your organization. While some influences are probably obvious—new software or technology, budget cuts, or a revision to a law that directly affects your work—you may need to think about other parts that are less obvious, such as different customer needs or changing workforce demographics. Take twenty to thirty minutes to think about factors in your organization's environment that you have observed. Then fill out the chart below.

TOOL 1.2 (*continued*)

Identify Factors That Influence Your Organization

Environmental Factors		Have These Factors Impacted Your Organization in the Recent Past?		Examples That You've Seen
Legislative or Legal Factors	• New laws • Changes to existing laws	Yes	No	
Social Factors	• Demographic changes • Changes in the workforce • Changes in the workforce's expectations	Yes	No	
Technology Factors	• New technologies • Existing technologies • Your team's understanding of relevant technologies	Yes	No	
Customers	• Customer needs that have changed over time • Customer needs that are changing rapidly • Customers that expect new or different services • Customers that expect individualized services	Yes	No	
Natural Disasters or Events	• Natural disasters • Diseases and viruses • Climate change	Yes	No	
Internal Organizational Factors	• Organization-wide reorganizations • Leadership changes • Policy changes • Budget or resource changes • New expectations about where and when work is performed	Yes	No	

What insights do you have when you look at your responses? Are there certain factors that have been really impacting your organization? Are there other factors that you suspect are influencing your organization even if you can't come up with specific examples? How might others in your organization be feeling pressured by these factors?

You may already have a solid understanding of the ecosystem in which your organization operates. Still, there are probably many things going on that you aren't aware of. The right next step, then, is to facilitate a brainstorming session with your team or a group of peers. If you are working together in person, you can use sticky notes and flip-chart paper; if you are working virtually, consider using collaboration tools that allow people to type on virtual sticky notes and post them to a virtual board.

Ask them to fill in the chart independently and then to share what they wrote. You might do this at a weekly staff meeting. Or maybe it's a good exercise for a team offsite. There's no right time or place or group of people to start with. The important point is that you start the conversation with the people you feel comfortable having this initial discussion with. You can always expand the conversation when it is appropriate.

If your experience mirrors what we've encountered over the years, you will find that many people list some of the same factors—and that's great. It means that people are seeing the same things you are, which tells you that there's some shared understanding of, and perhaps even predictability in, the environment. Some outliers may pop up, too—also great, as you will then learn about factors that you were previously unaware of. Your team may not completely agree on these factors, of course. Indeed, you might hear, "That doesn't matter," followed by someone else saying, "Well, it doesn't impact your work, but it sure impacts mine."

It's okay if people do not agree; just start with identifying all of the factors. As a next step, you can have people explain how

TOOL 1.2 (*continued*)

the factors affect their work, which will then help the team refine the list; through discussion, the team might realize that they have different terms for the same factors or that some factors affect only certain team members, given unique aspects of their roles. Later on, your team can prioritize which factors to tackle together and which might need to be tackled by individual team members. But at the beginning, we just hope you feel a sense of accomplishment; by starting to talk with your team about what's affecting their work, you will have started sensing!

TOOL 1.3: Analyze Your Environment

You're ready now to start analyzing the factors that you identified. In step 1 below, list a few of the factors you identified (use the previous tool for inspiration). In step 2, report whether this factor occurs regularly—hourly, daily, weekly, monthly, annually—or not. In step 3, list ideas for how to sense when the factor might occur.

Analyze Your Environment

Step 1: What activities, events, or issues have you encountered recently?	Step 2: Do these activities, events, or issues occur regularly or predictably (e.g., hourly, daily, weekly, monthly, annually)?	Step 3: What can you do to predict or learn when this event might occur?

For example, if input into the annual budget is something that affects your work (in step 1), in step 2, write, "Yes," because it happens every March. Although you know it happens every March, it might still catch you off guard, so this will help you to remember to start preparing in February. Your action item (in step 3), then, might be, "Add a task to the annual planning calendar that indicates to start preparing for the March budget request in February."

As another example, perhaps your division conducts strategic planning (step 1) and your team is asked to send a representative to a strategic-planning offsite. But the offsite isn't held annually; it's held only as needed. So, you would answer "No" in step 2. To anticipate that an offsite might be coming, you could list several ideas in step 3, such as, "Attend higher-level leadership meetings," "Read minutes from leadership meetings to see if there's any mention of the need for a strategic-planning offsite," or "Ask your boss if she's been in meetings where the need for an offsite is talked about." You also might ask some of your direct reports to be on call if and when the next offsite happens.

MAKE RESPONDING A ROUTINE BEHAVIOR

Just as with sensing routines, responding routines are everyone's responsibility. Different people will play different roles, but everyone must help figure out how the organization can anticipate and adapt when changes happen. Some people may respond by doing their work a little differently in order to meet a customer's unique request. Others may respond with a longer horizon, such as creating a plan to form a new division intended to meet a large increase in a specific type of work.

Responding can turn reactive if no one in the organization knows that something has changed until it has occurred. When something takes everyone by surprise, you have no choice but to rely on the commitment, hard work, and skills of your staff to figure out how to manage until an effective response can be prepared. Unfortunately, much reactive change often leads to stress, fatigue, and burnout as employees juggle their everyday responsibilities with the additional burden of a crisis. Reactive responses can also lead to a loss of trust in leadership, as people look to leaders to guide the organization to be more proactive.

Responding, ideally, should be proactive. If everyone is paying close attention to the environment in their sensing routines, then they can interpret signals and prepare an appropriate response. We recognize, however, that it can be hard to convince others that it's worth it to be proactive! In chapter 8, we present specific actions that you can take to encourage these routines, become more proactive, and then demonstrate the value of proactivity. Responses might include putting in place previously developed contingency plans as well as testing out possible responses. We expect that new solutions will not work perfectly the first time, however.

Experimenting and piloting are two good ways to learn more about the problem, refine the solution, and confirm that the solution will work. Experimenting—running short tests to quickly learn more about a problem, test an assumption, or try out a potential solution—is an important part of responding because it helps create solutions in a timely manner and ensures that resources aren't wasted on solutions that don't pan out. Piloting is another alternative to investing in a full-blown plan or project; it makes sure that the important aspects of the solution will work and are implemented the right way.

You might wonder if every event can be anticipated. Sometimes, people don't establish sensing as a routine behavior because they feel that it is not possible to stay aware of everything that could affect them and what's happening around them. While it's true that we cannot all pay attention to every stimulus in the environment, and there will always be some unknowns and changes in the environment that no one sees or understands, many events can be anticipated so that a response can be prepared earlier. And by preparing responses ahead of time, your employees learn more about the environment and hone their ability to innovate. If an event happens unexpectedly or differently than anticipated, employees who have been practicing their sensing and responding skills are better prepared to address it. They might save time by knowing which solutions won't work. They may be closer to the solution than if they were starting from scratch. They may know which experts—inside and outside the organization—to consult in order to get to a solution faster.

A response to a known event—a situation, challenge, or problem—can be handled with existing, stable processes. When a previously unknown event happens or is about to happen, the organization's flexibility comes into play. Small teams will need to come together to understand the event and its impact on the organization; these small teams should then conduct short experiments to find a response. For example, you might ask two or three team members to tackle a specific problem. That small team might start by talking to someone who has tried to address the problem before or to employees who have experienced the problem firsthand, to learn more about the problem. Then they might generate possible solutions that could be tested by one or two team members before rolling it out to a few others, refining the solution each time before making it the preferred way of doing things. Along the way, the team will likely try some solutions that don't work, learn more about the problem and other possible solutions, and then finally develop a solution that actually solves the problem.

You may have heard about approaches such as rapid prototyping, design thinking, or other techniques intended to tap people's creativity. These approaches are often run by small teams made up of the same people who sensed the new event and who have the best understanding of it. But a team might also need to add people who have specific expertise. In agile organizations, employees can self-organize to form these teams, keeping leadership informed; leaders may also take on the role of a team member if they have information and expertise related to the event. The teams can form, re-form (by adding and removing members as their understanding of the event shifts and new skills are needed), and disband when their work is complete.

Leaders can also direct teams to form. Agile organizations rely on a range of temporary and permanent teams, including task forces, tiger teams, and so on. Both self-forming and leader-directed teams should keep leadership apprised of their actions. These teams may need access to resources that only higher-level leaders can approve (yes, even agile organizations have hierarchies of responsibility). They may also need to rely on leaders to coordinate across the organization by connecting teams working on similar problems, reducing unnecessary duplication of efforts, and identifying others with relevant skills and expertise.

UNDERSTAND THE SEVEN LEVERS

To enable sensing and responding routines, an agile organization approaches its work very differently from the way a traditional organization does. Leaders have seven so-called levers that they can use to support timely and effective responses to changes in the environment. These seven levers are as follows:

- **Organizational structure.** Agile organizations maintain stability with a flat structure, which provides greater responsiveness than a more traditional hierarchy does. Small teams enhance flexibility by conducting pilots and experiments.
- **Decision-making.** Decisions in agile organizations are made at the lowest level, where expertise resides; as such, decision-making authority is delegated as much as possible. Decision-makers are expected to use an effective decision-making process, which includes gathering relevant information and informing others about their decisions.
- **Knowledge sharing and experimentation.** Data and information are shared as widely as needed in an agile organization. Teams conducting pilots and experiments share what they have learned to benefit others who are tackling similar problems.
- **Processes.** Processes, or parts of processes, that support predictable parts of the organization (like payroll or IT help-desk tickets for routine problems) are intentionally well-defined and stable, whereas those that support innovation or responding are intentionally flexible.

- **Roles.** People carrying out well-defined, stable processes have well-defined roles. People supporting flexible processes may have roles that are less defined, allowing them to engage in whatever actions their current situation calls for.
- **Leader actions.** Leaders in an agile organization, first and foremost, must create a climate of psychological safety. They must ensure that everyone feels that sharing information, contributing ideas, and conveying imperfect experiment results is welcome. Leaders must also ensure that everyone understands the organization's mission and goals, which allows people to take quick action, aligned to the mission, when needed. Leaders model and support working as collaboratively as possible. They also provide access to resources and higher levels of organizational leadership when needed.
- **Norms and expectations.** The primary norm in an agile organization is psychological safety; leaders must work hard to create a sense that it is okay, and expected, to share information or to tell others when something didn't go well. Additionally, agile organizations view employee development and learning as an investment—not a cost.

In subsequent chapters, we explore how you can use these levers to build your organization's agility. Rather than devoting one chapter to each lever, we've organized chapters by concepts that show you how to enact change in your organization. As such, some chapters focus on a specific lever, while other chapters address several levers. In any given discussion of a lever, however, we want you to think about how all of the levers are interrelated; after all, it's hard to address one lever unless the others are in place. For example, your team is not likely to share information if they don't realize the role that information plays in making good decisions. And they probably won't experiment with possible solutions if they don't feel that it's okay to form a small team to design and run an experiment. In addition, making progress on one lever can help you make progress on another lever. For example, you will see themes of psychological safety and team norms throughout the book. In order to make progress on levers, a team must have sufficient psychological safety as well as norms in place that support each lever.

Thus, the chapters appear in an order that we think will work intuitively for most organizations. We suggest that you approach your journey toward agility in the same order, but then refer back to the chapters, as needed, as you continue to learn and iterate.

MYTH: WE JUST NEED TO BE MORE EFFECTIVE

Sometimes we hear leaders say that the timing is not right for their organization to become more agile because the organization does not have existing processes that work well. In our terms, these leaders are saying that the part of their organization that needs to be stable is not functioning well—processes are not well-defined and are not getting appropriate results.

The truth is that the reason the organization is not getting the results it wants is because the organization is not aligned to its environment. Things will never slow down enough to be able to fully define every process and get to a state of stability. When the work environment was more stable many decades ago, organizations could improve their outcomes by documenting most of their processes and having employees carry them out as defined. Today, the organization needs to figure out which processes should be well-defined and stable and which should be flexible in order to adapt to changes. In subsequent chapters, we explore how leaders can set the stage for agility, addressing both the stable and flexible aspects of their organization at the same time.

MYTH: WE NEED EITHER STABILITY OR FLEXIBILITY—NOT BOTH

Some leaders we talk with say their organizations need complete stability, while other leaders express that their organizations need complete flexibility. The truth is that agile organizations find the right balance, or flow, between the two. You need elements of both stability and flexibility—the trick is finding where you need each.

In agile organizations, processes are examined in order to figure out where stability and flexibility are appropriate. And because needs change over time, those processes are continually examined and re-examined to figure out where stability and flexibility are needed. Previously flexible processes might become more stable due to the emergence of technological advances, a more skilled workforce, or increased risk. And previously stable processes may need to become more flexible if the environment affecting those processes has become more turbulent.

Evolving into a more agile organization is not a simple or pre-scriptive journey. When we started this work, many leaders and advisors asked us for a checklist of actions they could take to transform their organizations. Unfortunately, change is rarely that easy, and adapting to meet the demands of a complex environment often requires a robust approach. Fortunately, the skills you need to explore which levers will be the most impactful for your organization are the same skills necessary to meet future disruptions in your environment. As you start to use the levers, everything won't go perfectly. You'll need to learn what went well and what you will need to do differently, and then make adjustments and try the next iteration. It will help to focus on what you learned and why rather than on what didn't go well. Along the way, you will learn more about agility and what it means for your specific organization.

As you read the following chapters, be attuned to the little experiments you can try with your team and what small tests you might embark upon to learn more about your organization's strengths and opportunities to adapt to better meet the demands of your environment. But before that, in the very next chapter, you will learn the prerequisite to such experiments: you must enable employees to feel comfortable trying new things—by creating an environment that fosters psychological safety.

After catching up on her email, Blair finds that she has twenty minutes until her weekly team meeting. If today is like most, several people will join the meeting a few minutes early or stay late to tell her about their work problems. Maybe she could get a better handle on this new job if she made a list of everything that her team made her aware of.

She grabs a pen and begins to document all the items that come to mind, from slight changes to the regulations that her officers must follow, to new software that could automate part of her team's work, to a couple of new programs that constantly seem to need something from the contracting officers. A couple team members also once expressed concern about entry-level employees who wanted the flexibility to work in different time zones throughout the year, making it difficult for their colleagues to meet with them, even virtually. While this last issue doesn't seem pressing, if it becomes a trend, it could impact the team's ability to collaborate and the way employees are supervised.

Blair, list in hand, thinks, "Maybe I should start the meeting by having everyone make their own list of things that are getting in the way of doing good work. We could even share our lists. It might help us understand all of the pressures we are facing and make a case that we need to find a new way to work."

At the meeting, Blair asks her team to take turns sharing things that distract them from their work or keep them up at night. One person mentions a modification to a climate change law being considered by Congress; although this proposed law doesn't directly pertain to acquisition, some of the provisions would significantly affect most of the agency's contracts. Someone else mentions that one of the programs they support, the Bravo Program, has a lot more contracting demands than most others. Another team member says that the software they use keeps crashing. Blair starts with the obvious solution: "Do you call the help desk when that happens?" She then realizes that she knows how to address only one of the many problems her team is raising.

One team member, Barry, tells Blair that, two years ago, IT looked into the computer problem and discovered that the agency's computers weren't causing the problem.

"That's good to know, Barry," Blair says. "We just saved several months by not having IT reinvestigate this problem. At next week's meeting, we can talk more about how to figure out what to do about this problem."

After the meeting, Blair talks with Barry, who says, "I found it really helpful to think about all of the things that impact us. I wasn't aware of the new regulation under consideration, and Leila didn't know about the challenges I've been having with my customers in the Bravo Program."

Even in her short time in her new role, Blair recognizes that Barry is pretty outgoing, so she isn't surprised that he's on board with sharing his thoughts. However, some of the quieter members of the team might take a bit longer to be comfortable doing this.

Blair starts to think that she might be onto something by facilitating team conversations. If she can have her team continue the conversation they started, then they might be able to figure out which changes are always catching them by surprise. It seems like some of her team members are more interested in examining big-picture changes, while others are focused on specific changes right in front of them—she will have to figure out how to help them see that exploring both kinds of changes are important. Although everyone is already putting in extra time and effort, she might be able to find a way to get out ahead of all of the changes that are happening. It will take focus and united effort, but she has a good team who would be up for the challenge. And the payoff would be great. Right now, Blair's department isn't the highest performing. But then that's why Ms. Barton convinced her to take this job—so that she could turn things around.

TWO

Build a Foundation of Psychological Safety

Thinking about how much she appreciated Barry sharing his ideas with her after last week's meeting, Blair reminds herself how intimidating it can be to be open with a new boss. She recalls what it was like with her previous manager, Owen. Very few people shared anything with him, good or bad. Owen was as known for his quick wit in response to good news as he was for the biting quips with which he met bad news.

Blair drops Barry a quick note, letting him know that his input about last week's meeting was just the type of collaborative spirit she wants in the team. She asks what ideas he has for encouraging others to share their opinions about team dynamics.

An hour later, Barry appears in her office, eager to share his thoughts. Blair quickly learns that the department's previous manager, Gia, was not quite as dismal as Owen had been. Still, Gia hadn't fostered a workplace where people tried new things or shared more than they had to.

Barry tells a story about how, two years earlier, a few employees in the department had proposed a way to route their work more efficiently. Gia voiced her lack of enthusiasm yet still agreed to let the team put the new approach in place, without any testing or trial runs. The timing was unfortunate, however, because just as the new process began, unexpected legal changes required that many contracts be quickly revised, forcing the department to revert to the previous process to get the work done on time. Gia immediately deemed the new process a failure and, over the next couple of years, used it to illustrate the perils of trying out new ideas of any kind. Innovation in the department ground to a halt as the team kept their heads down and did only what was required.

Thinking back to her interview for this job with Ms. Barton, Blair now understands why Ms. Barton put so much emphasis on the need to modernize the department and address the programs' concerns about outdated processes.

After hearing Barry's story, Blair realizes that her team probably is not comfortable enough yet to really test out some new ways of doing things. She tells herself that, even though her leadership style is different from Gia's, it will take time for people to get to a state where they can really trust her and each other. But, Blair reasons, if she takes a consistent approach, she can get them to make progress. It will just take a bit of time and focused energy on her part. After all, they do have to get new processes in place to keep up with the volume and pace of work.

Blair tells Barry, "That story explains a lot about how the team operates. You certainly seem frustrated that you can't do things more efficiently to support your customers. How do you think the rest of the team feels?"

"I think almost everyone is frustrated with how slow and inefficient things have become," Barry answers. "A few of us are probably willing to go out on a limb and try something new. The rest will come around in time."

Before we get into the details of routines and levers, we need to cover the most important concept in an agile organization: enabling employees to feel that they will not be embarrassed, rejected, or punished for embracing new routines. Another way of saying this, using terms from chapter 1, is that employees need to feel that it's safe to sense, interpret, and respond to changes that affect, or could affect, their organization. This feeling is called *psychological safety*. Just as we feel physically safe when we make sure to lock our front door or not walk alone at night, we feel psychologically safe when we know that we can share our thoughts and ideas with others and they will listen without being insensitive and hypercritical. In a work setting, psychological safety is the feeling that you can take a risk when interacting with coworkers, direct reports, and others, and still emerge respected and valued.

This feeling is not a mere nice-to-have. Without a minimum level of psychological safety, people are unlikely to feel comfortable sharing information, having transparent discussions, or trying out new ways to respond to changes. Indeed, in many traditional organizations, these behaviors are not encouraged. Instead, employees are expected to do their job, with sensing, interpreting, and responding routines carried out only by those with formal authority. And employees who do try to engage in agility routines are often discouraged through formal punishment, such as a reprimand in their personnel file or a low rating on their performance review. Employees can also be discouraged in more subtle ways, through remarks such as "That's not your job" or "Let me worry about how this change will impact your job." Discouragement can be nonverbal, as well, such as an eye roll from a colleague, a shake of the head from a boss, or an employee suggestion simply going ignored. Further, staff members don't even have to experience discouragement personally to get the message—seeing how others are treated is often enough to learn which behaviors are not tolerated or valued. In other words, psychological safety is foundational. It forms the basis for agility routines and is a necessary condition for changing how the organization carries out work.

As a leader with foresight and an eye on the trends in your domain, your instincts might tell you to start by asking your team to pay closer attention to events and patterns that could have an impact on their work—to sense what's happening around them. However, if they don't feel psychologically safe, then asking them to engage in sensing may feel not only pointless but scary. To address this, first find ways to encourage a sense of trust. This is especially important as you are just beginning the journey toward agility. For example, when someone mentions a new piece of legislation that could affect the long-term prospects of your organization, thank them for sharing that information—in public if possible. When an employee takes a few minutes to talk with a colleague about a new type of customer request, let them know that's a valuable discussion. When a colleague sends you an article describing new technology that could improve your team's efficiency, tell them how much you appreciate their taking the time to send it—and ask them to present their thoughts at the next all-hands meeting. When someone with good intentions tries something new and doesn't succeed as well as they'd hoped to, praise them for the attempt and encourage them to try again, sharing their learnings along the way.

In a moment, we'll explore other actions you can take to build psychological safety, but first, let's take a moment to understand some of the science behind why our brains require this sense of refuge. We'll briefly explore why it's so easy to feel unsafe and then describe some specific actions you can take to enhance this type of well-being in your workplace.

UNDERSTAND WHY WE NEED TO FEEL SAFE

To get everyone on board with agility—paying attention to what's changing and what might impact the organization, initiating conversations about events that could impact the work, sharing information openly, trying out new ways to do work or improve productivity—everyone must feel that it's safe to do so. But what do people need in order to feel "safe" in the workplace—that is, to feel that it's okay to offer suggestions or try something new? Or that it's okay to give a coworker positive feedback for testing a new way to perform a task?

Research from neuroscience finds that our brains continuously and unconsciously scan our surroundings for threats. This "always on alert" function made sense thousands of years ago, when humans needed to be on the lookout for predators and enemies. Unfortunately for our coworkers and bosses, our brain is still always scanning for threats. Our brain remains always on alert, even though threats no longer come in the form of a wild animal or warring faction. Today's hazards are different—a micromanaging boss, a coworker who spreads gossip, and meetings where innovative ideas get shot down. So our brains are attuned to even small hazards, such as that coworker's furrowed brow when we offer an idea or an impatient sigh when we excitedly describe what we learned in a webinar. All of these modern-day hazards can make us feel embarrassed, ashamed, or like our thoughts are unwelcome or illogical. And more important, they discourage us from partaking in those behaviors again. That's because when we feel threatened, we naturally move into a self-protective mode of operating. And this defensive crouch reduces our creativity and willingness to take risks.

We can't help but feel this way. It happens automatically and usually unconsciously. It also happens instantaneously—neuroscience research indicates that it takes only 8 milliseconds to identify a hazard that triggers a fight-or-flight response. However, it takes longer—40 milliseconds—for the thinking and reasoning part of our brain to start working. The difference between 8 and 40 milliseconds might not sound like a lot, but it was a big enough difference to keep our ancestors alive. And in today's workplace it's a big enough difference to stop people from speaking up in meetings or contributing ideas during brainstorming.

However, there is still hope! A good starting point is knowing that it's easy for people to feel that they could be embarrassed, ashamed, or punished when they act with good intentions—and that it is possible to create a workplace that minimizes those feelings. Also know that, while you might have little control over changes that impact your organization, you do have control over how people experience those changes.

As a leader, your most important job is to create psychological safety in your own sphere of influence: your work setting. Although you will need to get everyone on board with the concept, it's up to you to start addressing it. You will need help from other leaders, both those with overt authority and those who lead from behind. Leaders at all levels are a primary influence over employees' sense of psychological safety.

You'll also want to pay attention to how coworkers impact each other's psychological safety. Praising one of your direct reports for offering to give a lunchtime presentation about industry trends will probably be negated if his coworker says, "That sounds like a waste of time." It's easy for just one person to tear down the psychological safety that has been carefully built up over time, so you'll want a cadre of supportive associates ready to notice signs of fear or withdrawal and to help you respond. You'll also want to try to encourage people to provide positive rather than negative feedback to enhance the feeling that it's safe to propose a new idea.

As you start to enhance psychological safety in your organization, remember to take a consistent approach. It takes time for people to learn to trust you and each other. Some people may get there sooner than others. How exactly do you know if your team feels a sense of psychological safety? Let's take a look at ways you can answer that question.

TOOL 2.1: Is There Enough Psychological Safety?

Figuring out if there's "enough" psychological safety can be tricky. Psychological safety is not something that you can measure with a ruler or thermometer. We've all probably had experiences at work that have enhanced or detracted from our own feeling of psychological safety. Those feelings can change over time, and they often depend on the situation we're in and the people we're interacting with. The same goes for your team members—they have all had different experiences that have led them to varying levels of psychological safety. For example, you might feel comfortable sharing offbeat ideas, offering your opinion, or trying out something new, but others may not feel that same level of comfort.

You might get a better sense of where your team is at by picking up cues. As a leader, use the checklist below to look for signs indicating your team's current state of psychological safety. Check off the statements that apply to your team.

Is There Enough Psychological Safety?

Signs of Low Psychological Safety	Signs of High Psychological Safety
☐ People share information with select others	☐ People share information with each other directly (e.g., at meetings, in person, in emails to the team)
☐ Some team members seem "out of the loop" and are left out of group discussions	☐ People build on others' ideas
☐ People shoot down ideas	☐ People respond positively to others' ideas
☐ Brainstorming exercises yield few ideas	☐ Brainstorming exercises yield many, many ideas
☐ Team members don't contribute equally to meetings or discussions; some members dominate while others are silent	☐ Team members contribute equally (over time) to meetings and discussions
☐ Decisions are attributed to politics or favoritism	☐ The team and leader allow and value everyone's input
☐ Team members show little initiative; routine problems are pushed up to the leader to solve	☐ Decisions are attributed to an effective decision-making process and the facts of the situation
☐ Team members show little empathy toward each other	☐ Team members show initiative by solving problems on their own (when appropriate)
☐ Team members blame each other, leaders, or factors outside of their control when things don't go right	☐ Team members show empathy toward each other
☐ Disagreements are not addressed directly and constructively	☐ Team members band together to learn from each other when things don't go right

Signs of Low Psychological Safety	Signs of High Psychological Safety
☐ Team members get defensive when someone disagrees with them	☐ Disagreements are brought up openly and resolved constructively
☐ Team members defer to the leader or perceive that it's pointless to raise another view	☐ Team members are supportive and inquisitive when a disagreement occurs

As you review your answers, you might find that you have some checks in the left column and some in the right column or you might find that your responses lean to one side or the other. You also might pick up on signs that are not on this list that speak to your team's psychological state. All of those outcomes are okay! No organization has perfect psychological safety. But that doesn't mean that you shouldn't invest time to enhance your team's feelings in this respect.

Use the checklist as a guide to know what to pay attention to when you interact with your team. Even if most of your checkmarks fall in the right column, be sure to pay attention to individual team members who reflect the left column. You might need to explore why some team members have a different experience than the rest of the team. Having even a single team member who doesn't feel safe can detract from your team's ability to function at a high level, so your role is to ensure that every team member feels a sense of inclusion. Over time, revisit the checklist to see if you're paying attention to the right signals and clues and headed in the right direction.

Now, let's take a look at some specific actions you can take to foster psychological safety.

USE THE PLATINUM RULE

Most people are familiar with the Golden Rule: "Do unto others as you would have them do unto you." However, when it comes to creating psychological safety, the Platinum Rule—"Treat others the way they would like to be treated"—is better. The Platinum Rule acknowledges that everyone is different and that we shouldn't assume or infer that others want to be treated the same way we do.

If you are just beginning the process of building psychological safety on your team, it can be helpful to spend time with team members individually to learn more about each person's communication and workstyle preferences. Then create time for the group to learn those things about each other.

Asking people about their preferences may seem like a simple, maybe even insignificant, action, but this process indicates to your team members that you are paying attention and that their needs matter. This conversation is helpful whether your team is newly forming or whether you have worked with each other for years.

You will probably hear some common themes as well as some individual differences. Even seemingly small differences that emerge are important to pay attention to. For example, most people want to be recognized when they do excellent work, but while some enjoy being recognized in a staff meeting, others prefer their boss pull them aside for a private, heartfelt "good job." To start to understand how your employees want to be treated, ask them directly. Consider framing the conversation something like this: "Thanks for making time for me today. I'd like to make sure the way we are communicating across our team meets everyone's needs, and I'm starting by polling the staff in person. Okay if I ask you some questions? There are no right or wrong answers—don't worry." If you get a green light, forge ahead with questions like these:

- How would you like me (or the department) to recognize you for good work?
- How frequently would you like to do check-in meetings (where we can talk about questions that both you and I have and discuss your progress as well as the organization's progress)?
- How do you prefer that we communicate? Do you prefer emails, phone calls, in-person check-ins?
- What kinds of questions or discussions do you think are important for us to have at our team meetings?

Engaging in conversations like this helps builds trust—and psychological safety—in a variety of ways. It establishes two-way communication and provides team members with the ability to give input on ways they would like you to engage with them. Starting an ongoing conversation about their preferences also demonstrates that you care about their ideas and views. People's preferences can change over time, however, so remember to also build in time for periodic pulse checks. And be sure to act on what they say—they will notice if the conversation goes nowhere.

Finally, another question to ask, and act upon, is in regard to feedback about your leadership style. Encourage your team to give you concrete, specific feedback on how your actions affect them. In chapter 1, Barry did a great job providing upward feedback when he let Blair know that making a list of all the changes the team was experiencing sent a positive message to the team. Blair's actions were beneficial, and Barry felt safe enough to give Blair constructive feedback when asked; hopefully, that's a start to Barry offering upward feedback when he sees the need for it.

Likewise, you will need to be receptive to suggestions for modifying your behavior based on input from your team. Showing that you are willing to listen to—and act on—upward feedback will not only help you develop as a leader but will also further enhance your team's sense of safety.

GIVE YOURSELF AND YOUR TEAM PERMISSION TO BE CURIOUS

Promoting curiosity is another action you can take to increase your team's sense of psychological safety. When your organization is getting hit from all sides with constant, unpredictable change, no one person, not even a leader, can know everything there is about the changes, let alone how to respond to them. An agile organization needs everyone to be curious about what's happening within and outside the work environment—and to be curious about how to design responses.

For a leader, curiosity often means having a thirst for information and knowledge that can guide decisions. Like many leaders, you might find that you rely less on your technical or functional skills and more on your interpersonal and leadership skills. You probably rely on people who have up-to-date technical expertise to balance your judgment and inform your decisions. It's probably also impossible to know everything that is happening across different departments and divisions, even when situational awareness is imperative. Although it can be faster to simply make a decision in the moment, without first looking for relevant information, being curious about what others are thinking and doing might help ensure that your decisions are not just well-informed but also defensible.

Constructive debate is another technique you can use to bring different perspectives to bear. Rather than pitting people against each other, ask some people to make a case for one solution and others to argue for a different solution. Start by explaining that your intent is to get them to think about the solutions from a variety of perspectives in order to bring the best solution to light. For this technique to work, you'll need to enforce the ground rule that people are debating the merits of the possible solutions—not arguing with each other; the goal is not to have one side win but to have the whole team win by finding the best solution or at least by identifying possible solutions to test. You also could ask people to debate (not argue) for the opposite side. This can enhance psychological safety by showing that ideas can be interrogated without assailing the person offering the idea. Part of building organizational agility is testing out responses to new situations and problems, which requires employees to feel safe sharing their ideas.

To encourage others to be curious outside of activities that you design for them, you can make sure that people understand the benefits of gathering and discussing information as well as trying out new solutions. For example, if you call together a cross-functional group to address a certain problem, you might explain that you are intentionally ensuring that multiple perspectives are represented—in order to yield the best solution—and then make sure that the solution is accepted by those affected. When doing this, your tone is extremely important. Rather than a tone of judgment, take a tone that conveys, "What can I, as the leader, learn from what you discover?" This latter tone is more likely to generate a rich set of responses.

Another action that encourages curiosity is to explicitly ask for people's ideas and input into problems and decisions. By doing so, you demonstrate your own curiosity while role-modeling the behaviors that you want to see in others.

When others then share their ideas and input, be sure to listen—really listen—to what they have to say. One way to do this is through active listening. Some tips for engaging in active listening:

- Listen while your colleague is talking. Don't think about what your response is going to be.
- Pay attention to your body language. Our bodies communicate a lot even when we aren't talking. If you can, sit facing your colleague. You might nod your head occasionally. Make eye contact, as appropriate. Don't look at your phone or watch!
- When your colleague is finished, pause. Use this time to ask yourself whether you need to ask a clarifying question or confirm what you've just heard.
- Confirm what you think you just heard by paraphrasing what your colleague shared. You might say, "If I understood you correctly, then this is what I heard . . ."
- Ask a clarifying question. If something wasn't clear or you would like more information, ask an open-ended question to encourage your colleague to share more.

Also, acknowledge the person's input, letting them know you value their effort. A simple "Thank you for sharing that" or "This information will really be helpful" can be powerful. More importantly, be sure to act on their input and acknowledge their contribution. Almost everyone finds it frustrating to take the time to research a topic or hunt down some information, only to have it be ignored by a decision-maker. Even if the information ends up not directly informing a decision, still take time to acknowledge the effort and value in their work. It is likely the information they gathered will come in handy at some point, even if you don't know when or how. You might affirm their efforts by telling them about a time when a team member found information that later solved a problem or helped identify a blind spot.

REWARD BEHAVIORS, NOT JUST RESULTS

Leaders in agile organizations reward appropriate, well-intentioned behaviors, even if the results of those behaviors are not what they expected. You might have heard sayings such as "Don't punish mistakes" or "Try to learn from failure" used to describe this concept. While we agree with the intent of these sayings, we believe that using terms such as *mistakes* and *failure* can still detract from psychological safety and are, therefore, best avoided when discussing outcomes. Alternatively, get in the habit of using the term *misstep* to refer to honest mistakes. Ask what missteps happened when the team tried the new approach and then ask, "What did you learn from this experience?"

Agile leaders do not consider something a mistake or failure unless an employee intentionally engaged in the wrong behavior. If the employee flouted a rule on purpose, for example, then you'll want to hold them accountable and make them understand that the behavior is unacceptable. Generally, however, we suggest that you assume positive intent. Reward informed, innovative behavior even if the outcome was not favorable, making your reasoning clear to the team member.

Very rarely does something go wrong because an employee was intentionally negligent. More often, you are not aware of the information that was available to the employee at the time. Learning from unexpected challenges can further refine sensing and responding practices by telling you which events to focus on or which steps might get you closer to a solution. In the end, spending time focused on learning is more productive and valuable than spending that time attributing blame. An agile leader distinguishes between the behavior and the results and, in this way, helps employees understand clearly what they are supposed to be doing.

Focusing on specific, desirable behaviors will help you with another essential trust-building tool: giving productive feedback. Often, people associate feedback with something negative or punitive. In an organization focused on increasing psychological safety, providing productive feedback is an essential part of building trust. By taking time to give feedback, you show people that they are worth investing in, which enhances trust. You also demonstrate that you are paying attention to their actions, which helps them understand that the choices they make matter.

One technique for building trust and psychological safety is to aim for making 80 percent of the feedback you provide over time specific and positive. You want to "catch" people doing things well. With this positive focus, you provide valuable information about what the employee was doing right and should continue to do. When you give feedback, be sure to focus on the desirable behaviors as well as any positive results. Those behaviors might include effective decision-making, improved outcomes, or contributions to the psychological safety of the team.

When you do need to tell an employee that she is not doing something right, try to present that feedback constructively and from a developmental perspective. A powerful formula for building trust quickly is to focus on a specific behavior that happened at a particular time and place, along with the impact of the behavior on you or the situation. For example, if a teammate is dominating the discussion at a meeting, you could say, "You know, at today's meeting, I noticed that you talked for about thirty-five minutes, which meant that we didn't have time to get to two important agenda items." This formula focuses on the specific behavior, not the person, which helps defuse the person's natural tendency to be defensive. After practicing this formula a few times, you'll probably find many opportunities to use it each day, mostly focusing on catching people doing things well.

Once you have established a strong relationship with each employee and developed the skill of providing feedback, you can give additional information about any negative impact that employees' actions might have had on project outcomes or other team members. When you provide this level of feedback only 20 percent of the time, employees recognize that you are still paying attention to their work and are focused on helping them build their strengths rather than looking for their wrongdoings.

Developmental feedback should also focus on behaviors or skills that could be helpful in the future. You could provide your thoughts on what those behaviors or skills might be, or you might ask the employee what he could do differently or how he could be better prepared in the future. For example, you might say, "When your slides were out of order for the presentation, the audience seemed confused and likely didn't get as much out of it as they could have. Given your career goals, you'll probably want to continue to develop your presentation skills. What ideas do you have for preparing for the next presentation? How can I help?" When used in this way, people begin to realize that you are paying attention to them—their effort matters—and that you are noticing the good things they are doing. This formula for providing feedback further enhances trust and psychological safety, which makes it easier when you need to give feedback in the future.

When situations rapidly evolve and change, it can be easy to make a decision that doesn't go well. As a leader, acknowledge that your instructions, guidance, and decisions are affected by what you do and don't know. Although it's easier to give clear direction when you know the situation, it becomes harder to provide clear direction when the situation is volatile and has many unknowns.

For example, a cross-functional team that is asked by a leader to find a solution to a problem will first need to define the problem. Rather than relying on the leader's understanding of the issue, the team may want to gather and discuss information (i.e., engage in sensing and interpreting routines). They may find, especially in a volatile environment, that the real problem differs from what the leader originally described. By understanding the real problem, the team is more likely to find an effective solution. If the team explains the redefined problem to the leader, who responds with, "That's not the problem I asked you to solve," then psychological safety will immediately plummet. The team will probably spend considerable time thinking about the solution the leader wants to see and not the solution that will solve the problem. In contrast, an agile leader enhances psychological safety by listening to the team explain the real problem and then praising them for investigating and understanding the issue before finding a solution. And an agile leader acknowledges that she doesn't know everything—including her own blind spots!

Finally, once people begin sharing their ideas and thoughts with you, make sure they know that you appreciate it. Thank them for their feedback and acknowledge their contributions and effort. When things don't wind up the way you or the team had hoped—a plan goes awry or a desired outcome doesn't materialize—focus on what can be learned from the experience, not on what went wrong. And, when you do get the results you want, be sure to highlight the behaviors that led to those good results and to celebrate that success collectively.

MYTH: TELLING PEOPLE TO FEEL SAFE WILL ENHANCE THEIR PSYCHOLOGICAL SAFETY

Leaders often share with us that, although they tell their employees, "This is a safe space," no one shares information, asks for help with a problem, or talks about what they've learned. Sometimes this happens because the team sticks with what it learned from a previous leader. Other times, the leader has good intentions but hasn't yet demonstrated to the team that it's safe, and expected, to try something new. An example is when a leader delegates a decision and says, "It's your decision. Just let me know what you choose to do." The team member then makes a decision, but it is overruled by the leader. Or the team member is asked to reconsider the decision because it wasn't the same decision the leader would have made; and when the team member comes back with a new decision, it is also questioned by the leader. While the leader might think he is showing high standards or coaching the team member to make better decisions, what he is really doing is teaching the team that their decisions, no matter how well thought out, are not good enough. Even though they've been told they are empowered, they begin to feel disempowered. Another way to say this is that team members have learned that it is not psychologically safe to make a decision, regardless of what the leader says.

The truth is that psychological safety is based on employees' experiences, not only on what they hear the leader say. Consider Blair's important realization as she started to work with her team: that simply telling them that they could share what they learned without fear or embarrassment would not help them do so. Rather, she knew that she needed to invest effort in demonstrating that they would not be punished or embarrassed. She would also need to demonstrate this using a consistent approach over a period of time to show them that they could trust her as well as each other.

TOOL 2.2: Actions to Increase Psychological Safety

As a leader, psychological safety starts with you. Use the assessment below to help identify actions that you can start to use right away to increase psychological safety. Check off the actions that you already do frequently, and then check off the actions you would be willing to do more often.

Actions to Increase Psychological Safety

Actions that Enhance Psychological Safety	I Do This Frequently	I Could Do More of This
I talk with each team member about our organization's mission and goals.		
I talk with each team member about expectations for the quality of our work.		
I take steps to make sure each team member understands why our work matters and to whom it matters.		
In meetings and communication, I make sure that everyone contributes relatively equally and avoid having one or two people dominate the discussion.		
I try to make sure that each team member feels valued and fairly treated, avoiding any implication that there is an "in-group" and "out-group."		

Actions that Enhance Psychological Safety	I Do This Frequently	I Could Do More of This
I encourage people to have open, honest discussions.		
When disagreements occur, I coach people to discuss the issues with each other directly and in a professional manner.		
I am receptive to people expressing their disagreement or discomfort with a decision or course of action.		
I encourage people to share constraints, both professional and personal, that they may be operating under.		
I praise people who ask for help when they need it.		
I frequently share praise and acknowledge others' contributions.		
I avoid using phrases such as "That's not how we do things here" or "We tried that two years ago, and it didn't work."		
I support decisions that my direct reports make, even if I would have made a different decision.		
When someone tries something new and it doesn't work out perfectly, I encourage them to try again.		
When someone tries something new and it doesn't work out perfectly, I ask them to share what they learned.		
When someone is skeptical about a new idea, I ask them for ideas on how to make the idea successful.		

As you read through these actions, do you see things you already do well? Can you find more opportunities to use these techniques? It would be hard to overdo any of them as long as you have good intentions. As you begin to put more of these actions into place, let your team know what you're doing. Your transparency will help them see that you are serious about psychological safety. Your actions—trying out new behaviors and learning from them when things don't go as planned—will speak louder than any lecture or speech.

After a few team meetings, Blair realizes that her team is not yet engaging in a lot of back-and-forth discussion or even gently challenging her ideas, let alone those of others. She wants the team to get to the point that they feel comfortable sharing their past experience and expertise, while helping them vet ideas before implementing them. Based on what she learned from her mentor, Carmen, she decides to start having twenty-minute one-on-one conversations with her direct reports to help them come to know her as someone who is genuinely concerned about their well-being and understands the challenges they face.

Blair puts together a short agenda and sends it to each person with the meeting request. She wants to make sure they know what the conversation will be about—that it's not anything punitive or investigative, but rather just a conversation to help her understand the business better. She asks them to come prepared to share three recent examples: something that they are proud of their team for accomplishing, something that they are proud of accomplishing as an individual, and a current challenge that they are working on.

Blair's first one-on-one meeting is with Barry. As she gathers her thoughts beforehand, Blair reminds herself to spend most of the time listening, not talking. "If someone does ask for my input," Blair thinks, "I need to remember to ask them what their thoughts are first." She also wants to ask for Barry's ideas on how to make their team meetings more productive. When Barry arrives, he seems pretty receptive to the meeting format. He gives some great examples of recent work that he is proud of, which Blair had not known about. When she asks about ideas for the team meeting, Barry tells her that the previous boss would often ask for ways to improve the meeting but then would never make any changes, so people might not yet be open to saying what they really think about the meeting.

Blair recognizes that there's a lot of history behind the team's lack of willingness to speak up—some team members just seem quiet, while others may not feel a sense of inclusion on a team that has increased in diversity of backgrounds over the past few years. It's not a matter of simply practicing good meeting skills. She decides to start with a new meeting segment called "What have I learned?" Knowing that it will take time to build trust and psychological safety, Blair starts off the segment at the next meeting by sharing what she learned this week. It's small—a mistake she made in pronouncing a senior person's name in a meeting. But she then explains that she will avoid future embarrassment by finding out pronunciations ahead of time. The second week, Blair picks an example that's a little more meaningful. She talks about a team that she was on a few years ago that was blamed when something went unexpectedly wrong. That event negatively affected that team's ability to make informed decisions, which had, in turn, reduced the team's productivity.

The following week, Blair opens up the segment for others to share their stories, and she is pleasantly surprised when several team members talk about positive outcomes as well as lessons they learned from unanticipated outcomes. Blair thanks each team member, explaining, "I am really learning a lot about each of you and how your experiences can contribute to the team. Sharing what you learned will help others learn from your experiences. It also helps us know that we can trust each other."

After a couple of months, Blair lets the team know that they will continue to spend a few minutes each week sharing what they learned, whether it's something that went well or not. And she says that she thinks they can incorporate their willingness to talk about what they have learned into other work discussions. "If we can talk openly about challenges, then I know that we can solve problems together," Blair tells them. "Each of us has a role to play in improving our team's productivity."

Blair feels confident that building up the team's ability to share without feeling insecure will pay off. She knows that she won't get the team to approach work differently if they don't trust each other.

THREE

Lead with Agility

After investing time to start enhancing her team's psychological safety, Blair wants to set the stage for the next step. The meeting a few weeks ago, where the team started to get a handle on the challenges at work—at least the ones they knew about—is helping her make the case that they need to understand these influences so they can figure out what to do with them. So Blair carves out a thirty-minute slot in the next team meeting to introduce the concept that might offer them solutions: organizational agility.

At the meeting, Blair quickly reviews the routine updates that she sent the team ahead of time. When it is time for substantive discussion, Blair asks, "What if we could find a new way of approaching our work? We've started talking about our environment and know that we are getting hit by all kinds of things. And we even have some opportunities we're not taking advantage of. We know all too well that our budget is not going to increase. If anything, it will continue to get cut. How do we manage to do even more work?" Blair glances at their faces on her screen—Barry looks intrigued, smiling; most of the others look like they are listening, except for Barb, who seems to be staring at her notebook. Blair hadn't expected that every single one of them would be on board. She has recognized, however, that some of her team are up for trying almost anything, while others consistently hang back, so she reminds herself not to push too hard at first.

She continues, "I've been reading about this concept called organizational agility. It's not a magic bullet or cure-all, but it might give us some ideas for how we can think about tackling our work differently. I am still learning, and maybe we could all learn about it together?" A few heads nod.

After a long silence, Barb speaks up. "Your predecessor made us learn a lot about employee engagement. We had to take training on how to be an engaging leader, set engagement goals on our performance reviews, and do a lot of things that took up lots of time. And now we're just switching gears? Forgetting all about that engagement stuff and doing agility now?"

Blair takes a second to gather her thoughts, musing, "I need to resist the urge to snap back with a quip about how I'm the boss and they should do what I say." She thinks back to her first mentor, Carmen, who talked about how leaders, especially women leaders, need to show toughness when someone challenges them. But then Blair considers how frustrating and confusing it feels to have a new leader who wants to go in a completely different direction. Remembering the progress that she's starting to make with psychological safety, Blair replies, "I think I hear what you're saying. You invested a lot in learning about how to engage your direct reports. From what I've read, finding ways to be more agile can result in employees being more engaged. What you've started with engagement can be really helpful as we find ways to become more agile."

Barry, always up for a new challenge, says, "I've heard a little bit about agility but am not sure what it really is. Just tell us what you want us to do. We can get that out of the way and then maybe have time to focus on our work, like we used to be able to when I started working here fifteen years ago." Blair pauses, then responds, "I'm glad you're on board with the concept. I know that it's not going to be as simple as a checklist of things to do or something that we tackle in a few months. I am just starting to learn about it myself. I don't have it all figured out. But I do know that, if we can learn about it together, then we will be better prepared to address whatever the future throws at us. All I'm asking right now is whether each of you are willing to learn about agility and to share what we learn with each other along the way. Maybe a good place to start is that we all agree, as a team, to share information with each other and work together. Leila, remember last week when you let Barry know that the format for the financial report had changed before he sent it to the deputy director? That's a great example of sharing information at the right time." Heads nod, and the meeting comes to an end.

"I guess some apprehension is to be expected," Blair thinks later as she works on a report. "But they seem willing to try. Hey, I did some things right this morning!"

Blair knows that in order to effectively lead her team toward agility, she will have to focus on her leadership style. She reminds herself that it's okay to not have all of the answers and that the leaders that she had early in her career had a different leadership style than she needs now. When Carmen was managing her unit, for example, it was easy for Carmen to stay on top of new regulations. The programs' needs were fairly consistent, so it was easy for Carmen to support them with a singular contracting process, adjusting the process only when needed and updating their templates and job aids. But, with Blair's department, things are changing rapidly and in complex ways.

Blair realizes that she doesn't know enough yet to stay on top of the multitude of events and issues by herself, let alone figure out how they might impact their processes. She also knows that updating their processes is not going to be as straightforward as making a couple of minor tweaks. To succeed, she must rely on her team to work together in ways they haven't before.

In addition to creating a climate of psychological safety, as a leader in an agile organization, your role is to help set norms for agility and to participate in the routines that enable it. Your role also requires that you embrace a different leadership style than you probably have in the past. Being willing to examine and adjust your behavior, while not easy, is necessary to lead in an agile organization.

TOOL 3.1: Examine Your Leadership Style

Let's take a quick look at your own readiness to change your leadership style. In the list of items below, place an *X* or checkmark along the line to indicate your views on examining your leadership style.

Examine Your Leadership Style

Item	Your Response
I'm willing to examine my own assumptions about how work gets done.	I completely disagree I completely agree
I am open to hearing what others have to say about how we approach work.	I completely disagree I completely agree
I am committed to exploring my own leadership style, even if I find out that I need to lead differently.	I completely disagree I completely agree
I am willing to persist with a new approach, even in the face of skepticism and setbacks.	I completely disagree I completely agree
I am willing to ask for feedback from those around me and to change my behavior to align with our new direction.	I completely disagree I completely agree
I am committed to using feedback to create a clear vision for collaboration for my team.	I completely disagree I completely agree

If most of your checkmarks are on the right side of the line, we are glad that you are open to ideas about how to lead and willing to try new behaviors. If your checkmarks are not all on the right side, don't despair! We appreciate your honesty and encourage you to keep reading to learn more about exactly what this new leadership role entails. By describing specific actions that you can take as a leader, we hope to make it as easy as possible for you to lead your team the way you need to in order to yield results. At the same time, we recognize that the hardest part of any change is to change yourself. You're not likely to convince someone else to change unless you are willing to change too.

Let's look at behaviors that you could start to embrace. If you are already practicing some of these behaviors, then we encourage you to continue them and then to find even more ways to apply them.

EXPLICITLY CALL FOR AGILITY NORMS

As a leader in an agile organization, you must set agility norms. *Norms* are expected behaviors. In other words, you must set clear expectations by explicitly asking for the behaviors that you want team members to practice to maintain an agile environment.

If you think back to when you started a new job, you might remember doing something that was not in line with your new organization's norms. For example, maybe you didn't know that you were supposed to agree with everything a senior expert said or that you had to have presentation slides even for an informal lunch and learn. You probably figured it out from your coworkers' shocked expressions after you voiced a view that was different from the senior expert's. Or maybe you were tipped off when you showed up to lead your first lunchtime session, only to get barraged with, "Where are your slides?" But if you were lucky, someone actually took you aside to tell you what was expected.

Without having clear expectations about how to behave, individuals are more likely to act based on their own views of what someone in their role should do, or even based on the expectations of their previous employers. Most times, people are not aware of how their previous experiences shape their current actions. As a leader, know that it can be helpful to surface these implicit norms by holding discussions with your team and making them aware of these past influences or assumptions; doing so will make it easier for them to understand why they might feel uncomfortable when you ask them to act a certain way.

Holding formal, planned discussions isn't the only way to set agility norms, however. Plenty of opportunities will likely present themselves throughout the normal course of work. For instance, others may seek your advice, either because of your formal authority or leadership actions, to help them make sense of what's happening around them at work and trends that might be emerging. This is a prime opportunity to facilitate discussion about agile behavior and how your work culture reflects it. It is also a chance to role-model what collaboration in an agile environment looks like; you can share your views because you have expertise and access to information that they don't. Conversely, they probably know things that you don't, so you can show that you respect their insights by asking them what they think. You can also ask them who else they might talk to, either to get more information or to help resolve an issue. And maybe best of all, you can let them know that the reason you are intentionally being collaborative is because incorporating multiple perspectives is more likely to lead to better decisions.

Another opportunity to set agility norms is when someone comes to you when a problem occurs, asking for the solution. Of course, if quick action will avoid harm to person or property, then make the best decision you can at the time. Most problems do not require immediate action, however, in which case you have the chance to ask what possible solutions the inquirer has thought of and how those ideas could be quickly tested. This also gives you a chance to reinforce psychological safety. If the team member takes you up on your encouragement, be sure to ask them to share with you and others what they learned. Even if the tests did not turn out as planned, they likely learned something that will guide them, and maybe others, to a solution.

In any instance, fight the urge to have all the answers. Keep your eyes always open for opportunities to let people know that they are expected to work collaboratively, including sharing information and the results of experiments. Point out examples where you see learning happening, especially when someone tries out a new approach that isn't immediately successful. Ask people how they can share what they learned, whether it is through an experiment, from talking with an expert, or reading an article.

Know that actively managing norms is an impactful way to help promote agility: if you don't actively manage norms, the norms will likely drift off course.

HELP OTHERS UNDERSTAND THE MISSION

Although employees are usually made aware of their organization's mission statement soon after they are hired, they don't always understand what the mission statement means for their day-to-day work. New situations—new legislation that could significantly add to the organization's already long list of responsibilities, customers asking for completely new services, advances in technology that other organizations seem to be adapting, or new employees who come on board with different levels of understanding about the organization's work—can make employees even more unsure about what to do to meet the mission, especially when the new situation is complex, not well understood, and stressful. It's one thing to read a mission statement; it's another to translate it into actions for a department, team, or individual role or to know when someone is charging ahead without realizing that their understanding of the mission differs from everyone else's.

Part of your role as a leader is to help your team members to understand the mission and the ways in which the change happening around them is likely to test its boundaries; then, you can work on helping them see how their roles actively contribute to the mission. What do those changes mean for how they are doing their jobs? Although you may not know how a change might affect someone's job precisely, you can have a conversation about it, asking helpful questions that surface their sense of the answer. You can also ask them what possible solutions might look like, which, in turn, may inspire them to test ideas to see what a sensible response might be.

By helping others clarify the mission and what it means for their jobs, you give them the ability to make decisions faster and more collaboratively when needed, both which help the organization as a whole respond quickly and more effectively.

EMPOWER OTHERS

As someone in a leadership position, you can empower others to make decisions by pushing decision-making authority to the right level. The "right" level is the level at which the person with the most knowledge about the potential effects of the decision resides. Delegating to the person at the right level helps provide the quickest possible response.

Pushing decisions up to a higher level than necessary means someone must take time to gather information (often by consulting with the person who has the most information), understand that information, develop options, make a decision, communicate that decision, and then hope it is implemented. This is usually a more time-consuming approach than simply asking the person with the most knowledge to make the decision.

At the same time, realize that you don't need to delegate every decision. For some decisions, you are still the person best poised to make them. You might be the person authorized to view last year's financials to give input for your department's budget. Or maybe you need to decide how to handle an employee whose performance has suddenly dropped off.

However, many decisions can be delegated to someone more knowledgeable. This does not mean that the delegate should make the decision in isolation. Any decision-maker must figure out what information she already has and what information she still needs to inform her judgment. She may need to reach out to those higher up to ask for input. She may need to reach out to people in other functions who also have relevant knowledge of the situation. And, once the decision is made, she needs to make sure to communicate the decision to the right people, including those higher up. We talk more about making decisions at the right level in chapter 4.

LEND SUPPORT TO—AND PARTICIPATE IN—THE ROUTINES

As a leader, you play a key role in supporting sensing, interpreting, and responding routines by reminding and encouraging others to engage in them. Everyone in the organization, including you, must embrace these routines. As a leader, you bring technical or functional expertise, experience, and insight into what is happening both across the organization and at higher levels.

There may be instances where it makes sense for you to take the lead when a small team is forming to make sense of the environment or test solutions to a problem—such as when you have the relevant expertise. You don't have to take the lead every time people get together to compare notes about the changes they see, however. Allowing others to step in and take a leadership role not only frees up time for you to focus on other activities but provides growth opportunities for others.

Sometimes, you may take on the role of team member while one of your direct reports serves as the leader of a temporary team. Other times, you may play an advisory role to a temporary team that one of your direct reports is leading: you support the team by helping them align their work with the mission statement, providing necessary resources, and assisting them in communicating what they've learned to other areas of the organization.

Agile organizations often free up staff by improving decision-making efficiency, allowing employees with the right expertise to improve processes and eliminate work that adds little value. However, agile organizations may require more staff, or even more financial and technological resources in other areas, such as planning and preparing for unanticipated events that would significantly affect the organization. Higher-level leaders in agile organizations place less emphasis on oversight and more emphasis on supporting those at lower levels as they introduce efficiencies and prepare for potentially impactful events.

TOOL 3.2: Support Behavior Change in Others
Getting an organization to operate differently requires getting individuals to do things differently. The first time—or the first few times—you do something new, it can feel unfamiliar and uncertain. Different people embrace behavior change at different

rates. Some people jump right in, try it out, and quickly adapt the new behavior as their own. Others may need more time to think about what they are being asked to do; they may watch to see how others carry out the new behavior and then slowly test the waters.

As a leader, you need to pay careful attention to how you support people trying out the new behaviors that accompany becoming an agile organization. You can help them learn and refine new behaviors by supporting them when they first try the behaviors and then as they become more comfortable with them. Read through the list below to find possible ways to support your colleagues' behavior changes. You might even think of additional ways that you can encourage them! Check off the behaviors you currently do, and circle those you would like to start.

Support Behavior Change in Others

Ideas to Support Behavior Change
☐ Suggest books, articles, or other resources to learn about a new skill.
☐ Ask the person to set a goal for the new behavior.
☐ Praise the person for trying the new behavior, even when it doesn't go perfectly.
☐ Communicate a need for changing behavior.
☐ Engage an ongoing discussion about what agility means for the person's role.
☐ Measure outcomes related to the behavior change, showing the person how the new behavior led to a positive outcome.
☐ Help the person find a safe way to try out the new behavior.
☐ Encourage the person to learn from their experiences.
☐ Ask others to recognize positive examples of behavior change in the person, such as sending a thank-you note or message of encouragement.

TOOL 3.3: Leader Agility Assessment

Leading in an agile organization can be very different from leading in a traditional organization. It may also be different from what you have been taught or have observed in other leaders. People in traditional organizations look to leaders based on authority rather than expertise. They may look to a leader to make a decision even when that leader may not be the person with the knowledge most relevant to that decision.

In contrast, to be a leader in an agile organization, you do not necessarily have to be in a position of formal authority. You can show leadership at any level and in any part of the organization by practicing the leadership behaviors described in this chapter.

The assessment below provides specific actions that you can take to enhance your agile leadership capability. For each action, check the box that best applies to you. You may wind up checking more than one box per statement, and that is fine! When you have finished the self-assessment, identify one behavior that you want to work on over the next few weeks.

Leader Agility Assessment

	I Could Do This More Often	I Have Room for Improvement	I Do This Often and Well
When I see evidence that someone might not feel comfortable sharing their thoughts, I take steps to address the situation.			

TOOL 3.3 (*continued*)

	I Could Do This More Often	I Have Room for Improvement	I Do This Often and Well
I check to make sure others understand the organization's mission, strategy, and goals.			
I share what behaviors and norms I expect from others.			
When communicating with others, I take time to explain things in terms of the mission and expected behaviors.			
I help others learn how to make good decisions by including them in my decision-making process.			
I let others make the decision when they have more firsthand knowledge of the situation, even if I would have made a different decision.			

	I Could Do This More Often	I Have Room for Improvement	I Do This Often and Well
I enable teams by helping them get the resources they need to be successful.			
I ask teams to keep me informed about what they learn from a pilot or experiment.			
I actively work to remove obstacles that slow down progress.			
I provide top cover to individuals and teams, allowing them to focus on the mission and learn from experiments.			

As you review your responses, think about ways you can continue to build your leadership skills. You can approach your development in a wide range of ways. You might start by observing what other agile leaders do and then try to enhance your understanding of these skills and apply them to real-life cases.

Review the suggested actions below and choose items to help you practice. Once you feel that you have sufficiently improved that behavior, revisit your self-assessment, and choose a different behavior to work on.

TOOL 3.3 *(continued)*

Other ideas for improving your understanding of agile leadership skills include the following:

- Find a colleague who is also developing agile leadership skills. Find time to share readings with each other. Set aside time to have a discussion about your takeaways from each reading.
- As you go through your day, identify agile leadership behaviors that people in non-leadership roles engage in.
- Choose a leader to observe regularly. Answer the following questions about the leader using the Leader Agility Assessment above as a starting place: What agile leadership behaviors do they excel at? Have they shown any behaviors that are not aligned with agile leadership? If so, what could they have done differently?
- Look for examples of agile leadership outside the workplace. Are there community leaders (e.g., a school principal, teachers, neighborhood association leaders, or local government leaders) who you think are positive examples of agile leadership? What specifically do these leaders do that makes them good role models of agile leadership?

Next, you can enhance your leadership skills by engaging in reflection. At the end of each day, spend five to ten minutes of quiet time writing or thinking about your day. While it might be difficult to block out ten minutes, you could reflect on your day while you ride the train home or go for a walk in the evening. Pick one of these reflection questions to address each day:

- What did you do well that aligned with agile leadership?
- What could you have done differently to show leadership in an agile fashion?
- Where did you see positive examples of psychological safety?
- What else could you do to ensure psychological safety?

At the end of each week, spend fifteen to twenty minutes writing about the agility principle that you developed the most and the principle that you want to work on the next week. Focus on one agility behavior to work on each week. Again, we know it can be hard to find time, but perhaps you can do a weekly reflection Sunday evening or first thing Monday morning. Here are ideas for additional behaviors to practice after you've worked on those in the self-assessment:

- Seek opportunities outside of work to practice agile leadership behaviors, such as getting involved in a professional association, neighborhood group, or volunteer opportunity.
- Practice asking for expected behaviors. For example, to encourage sensing routines, you might say to a frontline employee interacting with customers, "I would like you to spend a few minutes each day talking with a coworker about new needs that our customers have."
- When a team needs support (e.g., financial/budgetary, staff, top cover) to try a new idea, start by giving them a small budget. Challenge them to test the essential part of possible solutions to learn as much as possible in a short time. Ask the team to keep you updated on what solutions do and do not work.
- When talking to a team that is trying a new idea, focus the discussion on what they learned or hope to learn. Avoid using the word "failure." Try to have a conversation that revolves entirely around their learning.
- Keep an eye out for a situation where you could make a quick decision. When you find that situation, resist the urge to make the decision. Ask the requestor what they think the decision should be. Take a few extra minutes to ask others for more information and their views on the decision. Tell them that you would like to make the decision collaboratively.

TOOL 3.3 *(continued)*

- Watch for a situation where you are asked to make a decision but lack the technical or functional knowledge needed to make a good one. Identify someone with more knowledge and tell that person that you would like him to make the decision. Ask him to let you know what he decided to do.

You also could offer to coach or mentor another leader, such as a peer or direct report. In your daily reflection, incorporate your thoughts about how your leadership style compares and contrasts to your mentee's style. Consider ways in which you can support the mentee by modeling agile leadership behaviors and positively reinforcing the mentee's agile leadership behaviors.

MYTH: AS A LEADER, I HAVE TO HAVE ALL THE ANSWERS

Leaders often feel pressure to know everything and have all the answers. While there might be some reality to this kind of pressure in a traditional organization, leaders in agile organizations recognize that they don't know and shouldn't be expected to know everything. Because the environment is changing so quickly, there is no way a single person could know everything!

As a leader in an agile organization, you can do one of two things when faced with a decision: gather the information that you need to make the decision or push the decision down to the right person. If you feel that you are the right person to make the decision, gather as much information about your options as you can in the timeframe you have. This might mean reaching out to technical or functional experts for information. It might also mean reaching out to those above you or even to your peers.

If things are changing rapidly, however, you might want to delegate the decision to the person or people best suited to make the decision. They may be able to make the decision in less time than it would take for them to bring you up to speed so that you can make it. Share any important information you have with them that could impact the decision. You might know how much money is (or isn't) in the budget to support the decision, for example, or how much one option will significantly impact another group.

When leaders first try to delegate decisions, they can find employees are reluctant to make decisions. One leader we consulted with said his email inbox was overflowing every day with messages from direct reports seeking leader approval for minor routine decisions. It took longer to open and read through the emails and make the decisions than if the direct reports had just decided themselves. As a result, the leader had little time to focus on more strategic activities. He felt that he had told his direct reports that they had the necessary authority to decide, yet they still checked with him before making a decision.

The way forward was for the leader to stick with it and not give up trying to delegate while ensuring that direct reports felt safe taking responsibility for their decisions. He started by diagnosing why direct reports were not making decisions. Although he believed that he had delegated the authority to make certain decisions, his direct reports still seemed unclear about which decisions they had the authority to make and which ones they did not.

What were his options? The leader could meet with direct reports, individually or as a team, to reemphasize his confidence in and respect for their making the decisions that they should be. After that, rather than continuing to make decisions for them, the next time someone asked him to make a decision, he could take a moment to ask why the direct report could not make the decision, turning the responsibility around.

If direct reports are too fearful to make even routine decisions, the leader could ask one or two of them to discuss a recent decision at the next team meeting, during which he could demonstrate appreciation for their making the decision, regardless of the outcome. The leader could also ask a direct report to share a decision that did not go well and then guide the discussion around what was learned, while praising the person for making the best call at the time. In other words, this leader must address psychological safety, as discussed in chapter 2.

The leader also could ensure that direct reports had the skills necessary for making good decisions in general as well as sufficient information to make each specific decision. Empowerment is often misinterpreted as employees making quick, uninformed decisions. In reality, if team members do not have the necessary information to make decisions, the leader can help remove that obstacle by simply making sure they are receiving the information they need.

MYTH: IF I DELEGATE, THERE WON'T BE A ROLE FOR ME

Some leaders we have worked with seem reluctant to change their leadership style. While many say they support a collaborative, coaching-oriented leadership style and are no doubt already engaging in some of these behaviors, holdovers from a traditional leadership style often remain. One reason leaders seem to hold onto certain traditional leadership duties is because of the concern that "If I delegate, there will be no role left for me." The truth is that agile leaders still have a very important role to play—it's just different from the more traditional role. Leaders in agile organizations take on a more collaborative role, focusing on fostering a climate of psychological safety.

Changing one's behavior takes time, effort, and motivation. Trying new behaviors, especially when you are in a leadership position, can be stressful. It is easy to fall back into a top-down style when faced with time pressures, uncertainty, or other challenges. The result is that employees then wait to be told what to do, squandering valuable time. While waiting, employees may begin to develop their own plans or solutions, which are then wasted when the leader's plan is not relevant. All of this causes employees to become angry and anxious, which may make them reluctant to share information in the future. Therefore, when faced with a stressful situation, you should consciously refrain from reverting back to your old style.

In summary, as an agile leader, you will want to thoroughly examine your own behavior to identify traditional leadership tendencies that you can phase out and replace with more agile ones. Ways to support behavior change include setting specific goals for your own behavior, focusing on changing one behavior at a time, reflecting on your progress at changing behavior, and working with a coach or supportive colleague to discuss your progress.

Later that morning, another of Blair's direct reports, Ryan, sends a message that pops up on Blair's screen. It reads, "You know that program, Project Bravo, that is doing all of these services contracts? Well, I'm getting a bit concerned that if we start to see more programs taking that approach, then we might have a hard time supporting them. Is that really what we are supposed to be doing?"

"That's a great question," Blair types back. "We're here to support the programs and their acquisition needs. That's our mission. Just because we're seeing a program that has slightly different needs doesn't mean we shouldn't be supporting them."

Ryan replies, "OK. Barb is the one taking the lead with this program. Should I let her know that you said she should drop everything else to get this done? What about the other programs she supports that have been waiting for their contracts?"

Thinking quickly, Blair replies, "You raise several great questions. I am glad you're paying close attention to how program needs could be changing. That's good 'sensing.' Would you be willing to talk with a few contracting officers in your group and maybe a few other groups to see if they're seeing the same thing?"

"Sure, I can do that. But what do I tell Barb?" Ryan asks.

"Talk with Barb to see if she can find a way meet to Project Bravo's needs. I know you'll help her if she needs it. Just let me know what the both of you decide. Oh, and if we will really be seeing all of these new service contracts, don't worry, we will figure out together how to adjust so that we do things the right way but don't kill the staff with overtime."

Later in the day, Blair reflects on the conversation with Ryan. It was important to make sure he understands how the team fits in to the agency's mission. Unfortunately, she's seen other agencies where teams do only what's best for themselves, with little regard for a common purpose, and she's intent on avoiding that with her team. Blair feels she's on the right track by not stepping in to solve the problem that Ryan is starting to see. Although there's no immediate solution, she feels that getting Ryan and Barb communicating with each other will pay off.

Blair wants to make sure she's leading the team in a way that gets them to incorporate agility. She recognizes that, just as she is asking her team to engage in different actions than they have in the past, she will also need to examine her own actions, even if doing so doesn't feel comfortable at first.

FOUR

Make Decisions
at the Right Level

A few days after suggesting that Ryan and Barb decide how to support programs that have quicker turnarounds on requests, Blair receives a meeting invitation from Barb.

When Barb arrives for the meeting, she describes what happened a year ago—one program decided to take an incremental approach to its work, which meant that it needed a series of small contracts rather than one large contract. Then fast-forwarding to a couple weeks ago, Barb explains how a different program is now taking a similar approach. A little frantic, Barb adds, "They're just taking a different approach, which requires me to rethink things from a contracting perspective. Their needs are different, so I'm not sure if I should be supporting them in the same way or not. You know, when this started last year, your predecessor, Gia, told me to just do things the same old way and that if we didn't keep the programs in line, this new way might catch on. I really want to do what the programs need. They're my customers. I can easily adhere to the regulations and still support them, but Gia said that she and her boss needed to approve any contracts that were outside of the normal approach."

Let's look at decision-making next. Remember when we talked about agile organizations having the right response at the right time? Responding can mean making a decision to act or even to hold off on doing something. When change is happening quickly, decisions are often needed quickly, in order to allow time for the organization to respond in a timely and effective way. It's hard to have the right solution at the right time if your decision-making processes are too hierarchical or slow.

When something changes—maybe it's a new regulation or customers with slightly different needs (as Blair is experiencing)—it can take a long time for someone high up to recognize that those affected by the change need to know how to respond. Once the busy higher-up decision-maker realizes that a decision is needed, it might take time to figure out what information he needs, gather that information, and finally make a decision. After all of this, the decision must then be communicated to those who need to respond. Because this process takes time, responses come slowly.

When the decision does get communicated, it might be too late. Employees waiting for the decision may have decided on their own what to do. Or maybe they did nothing, which made things worse. And by making a tactical decision, the decision-maker had less time to focus on more strategic activities.

So how can you speed things up while still making good decisions? The answer is to ensure that the right people understand what decisions they are allowed and expected to make. The answer also involves making sure that those who should be making decisions feel that they have the authority to decide, no matter where they sit in the organization—executives at the top of the organization, middle managers, first-line supervisors, and individual contributors.

ENABLE DECISIONS AT THE LOWEST LEVEL POSSIBLE

What is the right level to make a decision? It depends on where the person with the most expertise or knowledge of the details surrounding the decision sits in the organizational structure. Decisions should be made at the lowest level possible. Some decisions are best made by those who are on the front lines with customers, while other decisions are best made by those in the middle or upper levels.

Even then, the person with the most knowledge of the decision details may not know everything he needs to know to make a good decision. The decision-maker may still need to gather information and figure out who else needs to be consulted. Having the authority to make a decision doesn't necessarily mean it should be a unilateral decision. Agile organizations, as we saw in chapter 3, approach work collaboratively; it follows, then, that decisions should also be made collaboratively to whatever extent possible. The decision-maker should try to involve others to the extent that their input and support are needed, balancing speed with information.

In addition, employees need to know what decisions they are expected to make. We find that sometimes people are not aware that they are allowed to make certain decisions, which often results in their raising decisions to their bosses. We've talked to more than one boss who is frustrated and overwhelmed with a multitude of routine decisions that the direct reports could be making but are not. Clarifying each team member's decision-making authority is one way to address that problem. Another way is to ensure that people feel psychologically safe when they are called to decide on matters that they are capable of owning. They must know that they won't be punished or embarrassed if they make a decision that does not turn out well for reasons beyond their control. (Obviously, someone who intentionally makes a bad decision needs to be held accountable—via a separate conversation with their boss, not in a public forum. But barring that, you should back decisions that your employees make, even if you would have made a different decision. And be supportive of them when they employ a good decision-making process.)

TOOL 4.1: Who Should Make a Decision?

When faced with a decision, our minds often immediately focus on the decision itself. It usually feels good to be asked to decide; we all want to feel knowledgeable and helpful. But to ensure that a decision is made effectively, it can help to pause and consider who is best poised to make it. Maybe you are the best person, or maybe it's someone higher or lower than you in the hierarchy.

Think about a particular decision that you are facing right now or one that you face regularly. To help determine the right-level person to make this decision, first ensure that a law or policy doesn't mandate who is required to make it. (In federal agencies, some decisions must be made by a certain person or at a certain level of authority.) If a decision-maker is not mandated, take a few minutes to work through the checklist below to help you figure out whether the decision should be made at a lower management or individual contributor level or at upper management level. Depending on where you sit in the organization you may discover that you need to keep the decision, or that it is more appropriate to delegate to another person.

Who Should Make a Decision?

Push the Decision to Lower Management or an Individual Contributor	Push the Decision to Upper Management
☐ The decision is routine	☐ The decision is not routine
☐ The decision is tactical	☐ The decision has strategic implications
☐ A quick decision is not needed	☐ A quick decision is needed
☐ Those with the knowledge needed to make the decision are at a lower level	☐ Those with the knowledge needed to make the decision are at a higher level
☐ The decision must be carried out by people who are at a lower level	☐ The decision must be carried out by people who are at a higher level
☐ The decision can be easily reversed	☐ The decision cannot be easily reversed
☐ A bad decision will have minor consequences	☐ A bad decision could harm people or waste significant resources

If most of the checks are in the "upper management" column, then push the decision up to the person with sufficient authority. If most of the checks are in the "lower management or individual contributor" column, push the decision over or down to the person with the most expertise. If you find that you have a fairly even mix of responses across the two columns, you might hold a quick consultation with a couple of peers who know the situation and can help you figure out the best level to push the decision to. They might even help you figure out the specific individual you need to make the decision.

Remember, whoever the decision-maker is still has the responsibility to involve and consult with others to make a good decision, and this includes higher-level decision-makers. For example, traditionally, executive-level leaders engaged in strategic planning without gathering input from lower-level leaders on the viability of the proposed strategy, but that practice doesn't fit into a more collaborative agile environment. While we're not suggesting that the responsibility for developing a strategic plan should change, we are suggesting that involving those who will have to carry out the plan will result in a plan that employees will be more apt to understand and rally behind.

MAKE AN INFORMED DECISION

Sometimes people think that pushing decisions down means that the decision-maker won't have enough information to make a good decision. However, being asked to decide doesn't mean being let off the hook for making a good decision. Decision-makers must still make good decisions by identifying options, gathering information on each option, and arriving at the best decision possible at the time. Although agility requires a timely decision, that decision must also be a good one, or as good as it can be in the time available. Every now and then, you might be better off making a fast decision rather than waiting to gather additional information. In those cases, you will need to weigh the risks of making the wrong call against the value that additional information could bring.

Another part of making a good decision is getting others involved. People in agile organizations work collaboratively and share information, which comes in handy when you are faced with an important decision. You may already know who to talk to, or maybe someone in your immediate circle knows who else needs to weigh in. Agility norms encourage people to come together to share information to make the best decision. And in collaborative decisions, you are not only making a better decision but also getting buy-in from others. That way, when it comes time to implement the decision, most people will already understand and be on board with the decision, allowing the organization to move even faster.

Of course, collaboration takes time up front, so you will need to find the right balance between speed and collaboration. But by pushing decisions down to the right level, when necessary, you are generally enabling decisions to be made faster, freeing up time for higher-level leaders to engage in decisions that are less routine and more strategic.

WIDELY SHARE DECISIONS

Once you've made a decision, if possible, share it—and the reasons behind it—with others. Most decisions can be shared. That said, not every decision can or should be shared. Personnel actions and decisions involving sensitive information, for example, can't be shared with everyone. And not every decision needs to be shared; it would be too time-consuming to share every minor or routine decision that you make in a day. We don't want your organization to get bogged down in everyone sharing every tidbit of information. So you will need to use good judgment about which decisions you should share and with whom—and that can take some practice. You might even pilot how you share your decisions by asking your colleagues for feedback.

We know that it's only natural to make a decision and then move along in your day. But by taking time to share the decision and to explain your thought process behind it, you'll set a good example for others, help them sense what's going on around them, and encourage them to practice their own decision-making skills by reinforcing psychological safety. People must have a certain comfort level before they will make a decision and communicate it to others; when psychological safety is low, individual contributors are less likely to make and communicate decisions because they think someone will criticize their decision or, worse yet, overrule it. So by sharing your decisions, you are actually encouraging them to share theirs, modeling the behavior that you want to see in them. And as a bonus: understanding why a decision was made helps people work together to act on the decision.

When you do share, remember that your colleagues don't know what you know; they might not even be aware that you made a certain decision. So before launching into a detailed explanation, consider just letting them know what decisions you've made, and then let them tell you the decisions they'd like to hear more about.

Finally, remember that decisions need to be shared in all directions. Decisions made at higher levels need to be shared downward, and decisions from the middle of the organization may need to be shared upward, downward, and laterally. People at lower levels also need to remember to share their decisions upward as well as across the organization. In most organizations, work is interconnected across departments and teams, so having visibility into decisions enhances people's ability to coordinate their actions.

We know that sharing information can be time-consuming. Especially when situations are changing quickly, it's easy to think that it's okay to make a decision and then turn your attention to the next matter without communicating what you've decided. However, others might need to know what your decision was in order to make their own decisions. So in the long run, it's a better investment of your time to find ways to communicate decisions now than to have to deal with a myriad of uncoordinated, uninformed decisions later on.

TOOL 4.2: Decision Log

As you go through your day, use the log below (or something like this) to jot down the decisions you make that you think others might need to know. When you see your colleagues, refer to these notes to remind yourself which decisions they might need to know about and how soon they will need to know them (e.g., immediately, by the end of the day, or by the end of the week). If you happen not to run into colleagues you need to share information with, make a note to get in touch with them to let them know about the decisions that apply to them.

As you start to use the log, err on the side of telling more people about your decision than may be necessary. Over time, ask for feedback from those you share with and refine your approach. You might also ask your colleagues to use the decision log to help them communicate decisions they've made to you.

Decision Log

Date	Decision Made	Who to Share the Decision With	When to Share the Decision	Check Off after the Decision is Shared
				☐
				☐
				☐
				☐
				☐

DON'T DEBATE, TEST IT OUT

One situation that inhibits timely decisions is when people debate with one another about options without arriving at a decision. You may have heard this described as "analysis paralysis." Sometimes this occurs when decision-makers avoid deciding. Maybe they feel that they don't have enough information or that none of the options are viable. Regardless, the result is often that people align into factions that support each option. Then the leader, after hearing each side debate and re-debate the options, despite having no new information, sometimes makes what she feels is the best decision at the time. This can unintentionally create a "winning" and "losing" side. People on the "losing" side then drag their feet when it's time to implement the winning solution; or, when the decision is implemented and things don't go perfectly (as is usually the case with something new), they convince the leader that the wrong decision was made, leading to its reversal.

To avoid this, we recommend replacing debate with experimentation and replacing the idea of winners and losers with an emphasis on collaboratively reaching a solution. How? Identify the options and ask people to work together to come up with a series of quick, inexpensive experiments to test out the essential parts of the solution. For example, if you are trying to find the best way to let employees know about a new internal program, you could test out two different communication methods, such as a story that appears in an internal newsletter and an informational session, in two different departments. Then measure (through a random poll or through the number of hits on the program's intranet site) how many employees in each department are aware of the new program. If you advocate for the internal newsletter approach and your colleague advocates for the informational session, it's okay if you and your colleague each try to make your preferred approach successful. Some level of competition can be productive, as long as the leader and group maintain psychological safety by not labeling people as winners or losers. Even those who advocate for an idea that is not ultimately adopted play an important role in uncovering the best solution.

The purpose of these experiments is to figure out quickly which option will solve the problem best and then to work out the kinks before the solution is put into place. Sometimes working out the kinks means combining different aspects of options to yield a solution. Then when it comes time to implement the solution, fewer things will go wrong. This cycle of experimentation and refinement often yields a better solution in less time than it takes to debate.

And along the way, people learn things that they never knew. They learn what didn't work and, of course, what did. And they usually find a better solution by conducting iterative experiments than by advocating for their preferred solutions in the absence of experiments. By maintaining a focus on the problem and its solution instead of taking sides in a debate, the group also comes to better understand the chosen solution and buy into it, which will help when it's time to implement.

FLATTEN THE STRUCTURE AND RESPOND WITH TEAMS

Delegating decisions is one way to make responding more timely. Again, when we talk about responding, we are talking about finding an effective solution in a timely way. Another way to enhance responding is to flatten the organizational structure as much as possible, as having too many layers of decisions slows down responsiveness. Although restructuring should not be done to address specific short-term changes, restructuring can help align the organization with changes that are predictable and will likely remain stable in the long run.

We've seen numerous organizations try to respond to short-term changes by restructuring. The sad fact, however, is that restructuring can take many years, depending on the extent of the effort. And when we talk to those at the bottom of the hierarchy, they often express a lack of support for restructuring because they know that it won't help them carry out their work any faster or better. In fact, restructuring distracts them, increases uncertainty in an already uncertain situation, and uses considerable time and resources. Processes often remain the same in the restructured organization, and roles often remain unchanged or become even less clear than before the restructuring. People resist the new organizational structure because they know that the best-case scenario is that it won't help them do their jobs better and the worst-case scenario is that it will make it harder to do their jobs.

Don't get us wrong—every now and then an organization needs to restructure in order to set itself up to sense and respond. However, restructuring is a lever that leaders pull too often, in our opinion, to the exclusion of addressing other issues head on. If you are going to restructure your organization, be sure to do it for the right reasons—to make the organization flatter and speed up decision-making. And remember that the other levers are available for you to use as well.

MYTH: AS A LEADER, I WON'T KNOW WHAT'S GOING ON IF I DELEGATE DECISIONS

Leaders are sometimes concerned that they won't know what's going on in the organization unless they personally make certain decisions. But the truth is that, by putting in place a norm to share decisions that have been made as widely as possible, leaders can have more knowledge about what's going on. And all decision-makers and leaders can have more insight into what is happening across all levels and stovepipes. Increased transparency puts everyone in a position to have more information and to know who else should provide input into a decision because they will be affected by it. The result of making decisions at the right level and then sharing them is that everyone can make more informed decisions.

> Blair sits back, thinking about who should decide how best to support each program. After a pause, she says to Barb, "You know what you need to do to support them while also staying in line with regulations."
>
> Barb says, "Yes, of course. Basically, instead of one large contract, they are asking for smaller contracts with more task orders. It's the same amount of work, just with a different cadence. However, if more of the programs start to go this way, not every

contracting officer will know how to support them. I think that's why Gia wanted to keep things the same—our process guides reflect the typical approach. If we changed things, then the guides wouldn't always apply."

"Hmm, I get it," Blair replies. "But we are here for the programs. We should be supporting them—that's our mission. Surely, they have good reasons for doing things differently, so we should help them. I also hear what you're saying about how this change could affect our group's work. I'd like you to decide how to best support Project Bravo's immediate needs. I will back whatever decision you make. And would you like to talk to the rest of the team to see if they're seeing the same changes? This might be a good informal leadership opportunity for you. Maybe talk to a couple of team members each day for a few minutes."

"That sounds great," Barb enthusiastically responds. "I'll let you know what I find out in a week or so." As Barb exits the virtual meeting room, Blair thinks, "That went well and is exactly how I want to lead this group! And I think it is what Ms. Barton is looking for when she talks about organizational agility." Blair sees how her actions are starting to come together. Telling Barb that she would back her decision made it clear that Barb was expected to make the decision while reminding her that it was "safe." Blair knows that Barb is in a better position to make this decision because she has all of the details about the programs' contracting needs; Barb will be the one who has to act on her decision.

"Making the decision for Barb might feel good now," Blair thinks, "but I don't know enough and don't have the time to guide Barb every step of the way. Barb is a great employee. She is more than capable enough to handle this on her own."

Blair did give Barb guidance on how to approach the decision through sensing—making sure Barb talked to the rest of the team to see if they were seeing the same shift in program needs rather than influencing the decision itself.

As Blair signs off on Friday afternoon, Blair's friend and former coworker, Luci, calls to catch up. Blair describes a conversation that she had with her boss's boss, Mrs. Banks, that morning, saying, "It turns out that Mrs. Banks decided last year—months before I came on board—that contracting officers have to adhere to the process guides. However, no one on my team was aware of that decision, let alone asked to give input! I'll need to talk with Ms. Barton about this on Monday. It doesn't seem very agile not to ask for input from the people who will have to act on the decision, let alone not even tell anyone that a decision had been made. I'm glad my team didn't get a reprimand. If they had, that would put an end to doing what our customers need!"

Blair recognizes that Mrs. Banks may not have made an informed decision, as she didn't take the time to involve the people who would be affected. But Blair also gave Mrs. Banks the benefit of the doubt, recognizing that Mrs. Banks could have made the right call: after all, it's possible there is something else going on that Blair isn't aware of. Even so, Mrs. Banks should have communicated both the decision and rationale to the contracting officers who were affected. Blair's strategy to first talk to Ms. Barton is a wise one; Ms. Barton may know the reason behind the decision. Also, talking to Ms. Barton will give Blair a chance to explain how easily her efforts to build up her team's psychological safety could have been negated.

After hearing about Luci's day, Blair shares again. "I did have one success today," she says. "Barb and Ryan started outlining a different approach for supporting all of these new requests. They weren't agreeing on the steps . . . and other people on the team started to take sides, so Barb and Ryan asked me to decide. I don't know as much about those regulations as they do, or whether our software would even support a different process, so I asked them to walk through a couple of previous requests to test out which steps will work best. I can't wait to find out what they learn!" Blair is pleased with her progress on delegating decisions, knowing that it will still take time to develop her team's decision-making skills.

FIVE

Promote Collaborative Learning

Barb joins the virtual meeting feeling a little nervous as she fills Blair in on two recent events. First, Barb describes how she was working in the office the other day and spoke with a couple of other team members to learn more about how they support their customers and what changes to the contracting cadence might mean for their work. The discussion was impromptu, and a few minutes in, another supervisor walked past the small meeting room they had stepped into and made an off-the-cuff comment: "Does Blair know that you're just having chat sessions while the programs are waiting for you to finish their market research and issue RFPs?"

Next, Barb describes a talk that she had with another team member, Vincent. "I've touched base with everyone on the team to find out how many of us are starting to see customers with different needs than in the past. When I talked to Vincent, he was adamant that nothing had changed and everything was staying the same. He said that it took him a long time to learn the standard process, it wasn't broken, and he didn't think anything needed to be fixed except for just working harder to get through the backlog. But..."

Blair senses Barb's hesitancy and tries to reassure her: "But...? It's okay, Barb. I need to know what happened so that we can figure this out together. I know we're not performing well sometimes, and I need help learning where and why that's occurring."

Barb continues, "In addition to talking to the team, I thought I should reach out to a few customers. I have a friend working on Project Charlie, so I gave him a quick call. It turns out that Vincent supports that project. Well, my friend said that Vincent insisted on following the standard process, which caused a serious delay in getting needed contractor support. So, now, I feel like I'm tattling on Vincent!"

Blair is pleased that Barb felt comfortable enough to share this with her and is not totally surprised that Vincent was not open to new approaches. Blair feels that all of the time she devoted to holding one-on-one conversations has enhanced each team member's comfort level in sharing with her individually, and she starts to ponder ways to get the team to have these conversations with each other—such as asking Barb to let Vincent know that his actions delayed the project.[1]

People in agile organizations are constantly learning. And that learning can come in many different forms. Sometimes learning is a purely individual activity—such as when you take a class or read a book. Other times, it is collaborative—working together to learn new things (such as when a small group conducts an experiment or attends an instructional webinar) and then applying those things to the organization's work. But the first step toward any type of learning in an agile organization is something we've already talked about: sharing information and decisions.

Without sharing, the information that you collect when sensing is essentially just a bunch of data points or facts. It doesn't become learning until you interpret what those points or facts mean for your organization and then think or talk about it with colleagues. Even when you take the initiative to learn something on your own, the real benefit comes from sharing what you learned so that others in the organization come to the same level of understanding and can apply that learning together. That's not to say you should try to repeat to your teammates everything you learned when you took a

---

1. Jennifer Myers contributed to this chapter.

training class or read a book on a technical subject. However, you would do well to share the key takeaways that might be relevant to your work and then to collaborate with your teammates to apply that learning to the team's work.

Of course, you and your team must have a sufficient level of psychological safety before you feel comfortable learning together. But once you do, learning will happen in many different ways. It will come from sensing and interpreting what's going on around you. It will come from pilots and experiments with your products and services. And it will come from your own leadership actions. As everyone gains a genuine desire to learn more, it will also come from discussions, constructive debates, shared decisions, and—as we saw in the last chapter with Blair—even post-work conversations with friends.

KNOWLEDGE SHARING

While sharing knowledge is crucial for learning, not every piece of knowledge can or should be shared. So exactly what kinds of things should be shared? And what is the best way to share them? Distinguishing the type of knowledge you're dealing with can help you find the right way to share it. Knowledge can belong to one of three types: explicit, implicit, or tacit.

Explicit knowledge is easily documented and can be shared widely without interacting with the expert; for example, processes and guidelines can be documented by experts, distributed to many others, and retained over time in a knowledge repository, such as a shared drive or database.

Conversely, *implicit knowledge* is acquired through your own experience or through direct contact with an expert, such as when you reach out to a colleague who has particular expertise to get help with a question or problem. Generally, implicit knowledge comes into play when the information to be shared is highly complex. Maybe you're trying to apply a solution described in a manual or textbook, for instance, and you discover that your situation is slightly different or more complicated than the one depicted in the book; finding a coworker who has tackled similar problems might help you uncover ways to adapt the prescribed solution or find hidden steps that you weren't familiar with. Implicit knowledge is best shared through a verbal exchange that includes the expert giving a demonstration and then assisting you (and others, in the case of training) as you try to apply the knowledge.

Finally, *tacit knowledge* is embedded in the expert's experiences, which makes it hard to access and capture. It's the intuitive part of expertise that is now second nature to the expert. Experts may take their knowledge for granted and not fully appreciate the value of their repeated experiences. This type of knowledge is best shared through long-term on-the-job training or apprenticeship programs.

Learning sometimes also happens when an employee makes a misstep, which is an honest or unintentional mistake. Agile organizations pay close attention to missteps because they often highlight areas where processes and procedures can be clarified or improved and where employees can enhance their skills. A misstep might show up in many different ways. It might be a unique case that can't be processed in the same way as routine cases. It might be an employee who misinterprets a communication or forgets to perform an important part of a process. It might be someone who is missing a key piece of information. And because the organization's situation is constantly changing in new and complex ways, it might be that the previous way of accomplishing work no longer applies—only you didn't know it until it was too late. Of course, if someone intentionally makes a mistake, that should be addressed in a manner reflecting the severity of the act and in a way that promotes psychological safety (e.g., discussing it with the employee in private—not in public).

Another way that learning occurs is when someone senses contradictory to commonly held knowledge and feels safe enough to share it. This might show up as, "You know, we've been assuming that our customers will need more of this certain service that we provide, but I've been seeing customers who are finding ways to get around needing that service." While it's often human nature to disregard information that contradicts what we believe, psychological safety, along with norms about sharing information, provides the right setting for people to pay attention to such information. Unfortunately, it's all too common to respond to a statement like that with, "Well, I'm going to keep my mouth shut. The director just invested a lot of money building up that service, and I'm not going to be the one to say that it was a bad move."

Of course, psychological safety plays an important role in knowledge sharing. That's why fostering an environment where people feel comfortable sharing their constructive views is essential in an agile organization. If there is enough psychological safety, employees will more likely share information or decisions, even if they don't see how it's immediately relevant. This type of sharing often shows up in the form of "I'm not sure if this means anything, but I just found out . . ." Agile organizations expect people to spend time in discussions like this; they view it as an investment (more on that in chapter 9). Although we don't want you to spend time on fruitless discussions, it's hard to know whether some new piece of information is relevant unless you first share and discuss it. Then the team can decide, after a few minutes, that the information is not immediately relevant and move on to the next topic. Although not every discussion will lead to a great insight that heads off a huge problem, sometimes that does happen. And the few minutes invested in each of these discussions often pays off many times over. So in the long term, agile organizations benefit from these discussions.

SET NORMS FOR INFORMATION SHARING AND INTERPRETING

We talked, back in chapter 3, about using your role as a leader to set new norms. Now let's take a look at setting norms for information sharing and interpreting and see how those norms are crucial for an agile organization.

Unfortunately, many organizations try to restrict the sharing of information while also limiting how much time people spend figuring out what information means to the organization. In the short run, this can make the organization more efficient because it frees up time to focus on the job at hand. To keep someone from being injured or to prevent a significant loss of a resource, it is appropriate for an organization to make a quick decision, examining only pertinent data. Other situations also demand that information should not be shared, such as when dealing with sensitive, classified, or personnel information. But over time, restricting information is a shortsighted way of operating because it puts the organization into reactive mode while quashing its ability to be proactive. It also detracts from psychological safety as employees get the message that it's not okay to share information; as a result, they often feel conflicted and frustrated when they sense something that could negatively affect the organization but know they will be reprimanded for alerting others.

Even in an agile organization, however, team members can all have very different ideas about what information is and is not okay to share, because they've come from different organizations and had different leaders. As a leader, then, it's your job to find ways to make sure they know what is okay to do and what they are expected to do.

It might sound easy to simply tell your team, "Be sure to share information" and "It's okay to spend a few minutes talking about what that information means for our work." While those statements are probably a good starting point, it's best to let them lead you to a deeper discussion about norms with your team. Consider holding a norm-setting session where you collaboratively come up with these norms. That will give your team time to ask questions about what you really mean and come to a shared understanding about what is expected. And having them help come up with the norms will ensure that they buy in to them. Your team might even add specifics about what information is okay to share and with whom. While it's important that the team phrase the norms in their own words, here are some examples of norms that you might expect to see:

- Everyone should feel comfortable sharing information, even if it contradicts what we thought we knew.
- Everyone is expected to share information and build interpersonal connections within our team as well as with others in our team and organization (barring security, legal, or personnel constraints).

- If you see a colleague struggling with a problem, ask if they'd like some assistance and share what you know if you think it might help them.
- If you run across information that might help someone solve a problem, avoid a problem, or generally improve how their work is done, push that information out to them.
- It's okay to ask for information when you need it.
- It's not okay to intentionally withhold information.
- Information belongs to the organization, not to individuals; no individual "owns" information.
- Try to provide information in a form that is useful and relevant to the person who needs it.
- It's okay to take time interpreting what data or information mean for your job, for the team's work, and for the organization's mission.

Even after norm-setting, not all team members will feel comfortable sharing information at first, and those who do might initially feel uncomfortable. So remember to keep an eye out for the behaviors that you want to see, let them know that you've noticed those behaviors, and reinforce them with a "Thank you for sharing that." Even if they're just asking a coworker to help them interpret information, for example, you can say, "I'm glad you took a few minutes to talk to someone else to figure out what this news means." Offer praise even if the information turns out not to be immediately relevant.

After a while, those who have started to share will become more comfortable doing so, and those who have not shared will be encouraged by the positive feedback their colleagues receive before possibly giving it a try themselves. In due time, these new norms will become second nature to your team, and that will make it even easier when new team members are brought on board. Even if new-hires came from an organization where information was not shared or interpreted and they feel unsure at first, they will more quickly and easily learn that you expect them to share if doing so is just business as usual for the rest of the team.

Over time, you may not need to notice and reinforce every instance of sharing that you see, but you should still monitor the norm to make sure your team isn't reverting to previous habits. And as information sharing and interpreting becomes "how we do things around here," you should start seeing your team make better, more informed decisions. You might even start seeing decisions being made faster, because people have information at the right time: you might have fewer bottlenecks that were caused by someone hoarding information, for example, or employees may just feel more comfortable making the decisions you've delegated to them because they know they have the information they need. You are also likely to see more proactive responses as people share information before it's needed rather than waiting for a problem to occur. As a result, you might experience fewer instances of being caught by surprise or having decisions not work out because of a blind spot. Information sharing and interpreting, in turn, feed into piloting and experimenting, which helps your team further learn and develop their skills. Sharing problems that happen in an experiment, for example, is a great way to pinpoint areas where a process can be improved.

As with most changes you make with your team, not everything will go perfectly. One pitfall to watch out for is "I need to go to a lot of meetings so that I know what's going on." When one person starts asking to be included in meetings simply to "know what's going on," that can quickly become a norm. Soon, other people might start asking to go to meetings, and suddenly your whole team will do nothing but go to meetings. This behavior can be an indicator that information and decisions are not shared widely enough. Meetings are generally more effective when information is shared ahead of time, such as in short, digestible reports or pre-reads, so that valuable meeting time can focus on making decisions. Only those who need to weigh in on the decisions being discussed need to attend. After the meeting, decisions should be shared as widely as possible, including a brief statement about the rationale for the decision.

A different pitfall that we've seen is when someone feels that they need to share every detail with others. Generally, people who share too much information have good intentions and are simply trying to be transparent, but the result can be that they're wasting others' time with too many details or too much irrelevant information. When we suggest that information be shared widely, we mean that people should simply have access to information when they need it. Sometimes that means telling people what information is available and who to contact to find out more. Having a norm that it's okay to request information also works well, but only if people know what information exists. This balance between oversharing versus undersharing is something you will have to constantly monitor.

Still another pitfall is when a situation unfolds quickly and people feel they don't have the time to stop and share the relevant information—or they make a decision without seeking the relevant information. Not sharing information, however, can hurt others who need it. We're not suggesting that you put in extra hours writing emails or schedule additional meetings to convey information. And we're not trying to imply that you ignore an urgent situation. Instead, we are asking that you use good judgment while still adhering to information-sharing norms. It's perfectly reasonable, for example, to wait until you have attended to a higher priority or urgent situation before you share news, assuming that someone else doesn't urgently need it. Here are a few ideas for how to share information in a timely manner:

- Use the decision log in chapter 4 to remember to share decisions, expanding its use to include other information (not just decisions) that you want to share.
- Delegate some of your work to a direct report, which would give her a chance to learn a new skill while freeing up time for you to share information.
- Get help from a colleague who is less busy, perhaps rotating certain duties to help free up each other's time for information sharing.
- Devote a small amount of time during meetings to sharing quick updates, timely news, and an overview of new information that

people can look into; ask those who are interested to meet offline to interpret the information.

- During meetings, ask one person to communicate decisions made in the meetings to people who need it but are not in attendance; this will prevent duplicated efforts caused by expecting each meeting attendee to pass information along.
- Avoid spending time filtering, summarizing, or rewriting information to share with others; instead, pass along or make available "as-is" meeting notes or pre-reads.
- Use technology to facilitate efficient information sharing; this could be as straightforward as creating a list-serve of names when forwarding information to others or it could involve more complicated and sophisticated technology tools.

Many organizations expect managers to perform technical or functional work aligned with their expertise in addition to supervising employees. Sometimes it's easy for managers to receive the message that managing is not their highest priority or that ensuring their direct reports' success is not valued. We view setting norms and ensuring that the right information gets shared at the right time as an important part of a manager's job. Your team will be much more effective if you find ways for them to know what's going on within your team as well as elsewhere in the organization.

Sharing and interpreting information is an ongoing activity. It's not something that should be done for a short period and then stopped. And it's not something that should be done just intermittently, whether once a year or once a week. Although some information may lend itself to being shared according to a predictable schedule, other information may need to be shared in between those predictable times. Remember, the important part is to get information to the right people when they need it, not necessarily when it's convenient for you. That said, figuring out who needs what information and when is an important part of your role. As part of that, you may need to ask for and act on feedback about your information-sharing practices.

TOOL 5.1: What Are Your Organization's Information-Sharing Norms?

If you've already held the norm-writing session suggested at the beginning of the previous section, you can use the table below to assess your team's progress in adhering to the information-sharing norms you documented. List your team's norms in the first column. Then ask each team member to complete the table individually, followed by a team discussion about how well each norm is followed. If even one person thinks that a norm is not followed consistently, have a discussion to understand why that team member has that perception. Then talk further about what can be done to follow that norm.

Remember that you want team members to feel that it's psychologically safe to disagree with you or the rest of the team. One team member may have different perceptions than everyone else, or each person on your team may have a different view. That's okay! In fact, that's the purpose of the tool—to understand where you and your team can enhance your understanding about what is expected.

What Are Your Organization's Information-Sharing Norms?

Our Information-Sharing Norms	Not Followed	Followed Sometimes	Followed Consistently

TURN MEETINGS INTO MEANINGFUL DISCUSSIONS

Meetings can be a productive, purposeful way to share information and create new insights. They can also be a waste of resources and a drag on your time. Although holding an efficient meeting will not automatically transform your organization into an agile one, it is a necessary first step to holding meaningful discussions. Being intentional about how you set up and run your meetings, especially those that happen on a regular basis, can be an easy and relatively inexpensive way to boost your agility and productivity. With your team, develop meeting norms that feel relevant and helpful. The goal is not to create overly formal meetings but to create a meeting format that supports your team in having productive conversations. A few straightforward meeting norms could include the following:

- Have an agenda that describes the decisions that need to be made.
- Provide information ahead of time—and expect attendees to read it—so that the meeting focuses on discussions that arrive at a decision.
- Invite only those needed to weigh in on the decision.
- Decide who will inform others about decisions made.
- Capture decisions and action items in a central location, providing access to as many people as possible.
- Don't meet unless you need to; cancel the meeting if there are no decisions needed.
- Schedule each meeting for only as much time as needed, whether that means a five-minute stand-up meeting or a ninety-minute meeting; avoid scheduling every meeting for sixty minutes just because that's the default on your calendar.
- Schedule additional short meetings if a decision is needed before the next meeting; be sure to include everyone who is needed for that decision in the meetings and, once the decision is made, inform those who did not need to attend and weigh in.
- Set rules that address how many team members must be present for a decision to be made.

As with other norms, ask your team to write their own set of meeting protocols. Finally, remember not to get bogged down in work that provides little value, such as overly detailed meeting agendas, verbatim meeting notes, and lengthy write-ups about decisions and action items. We suggest using a "light" approach to this documentation. A meeting agenda, for example, can be as straightforward as a list of needed decisions that appears in the meeting invitation. The agenda can then become the basis for tracking decisions by simply adding a few explanatory bullets, along with the decision and action items. Further, many organizations are moving away from complex sets of policies, which are often organized by function and difficult to maintain as situations change. Instead, some organizations are now providing "playbooks" and "game plans," organized in ways that are meaningful to employees and provide helpful guidance while adhering to law and policy; they are updated based on employee feedback as well as changing situations.

An additional tip for fostering meaningful meeting discussions is to include all meeting participants in the discussion and give them an equal voice. Try to avoid making decisions in the "meeting after the meeting" or during side discussions, as this can reduce psychological safety by leaving some participants out of the decision-making process. The round-robin technique is one way to make sure every meeting attendee has a voice and a chance to weigh in on the discussion. Rather than have a free-for-all discussion, in which a few attendees often dominate the conversation, it can be much more efficient to ask each attendee, one at a time, to make one point. In meetings with both in-person and virtual attendees, you can reinforce a sense of inclusion by asking any remote attendees to respond first.

Finally, when making decisions, use straightforward voting techniques. One example technique is called "fist-to-five." Fist-to-five is a low-tech way of voting or showing agreement (or disagreement) with a statement. People vote by holding up any number of fingers—from zero (by making a fist) to five—at the same time. A fist or one finger means you don't agree and cannot live with the decision being proposed; five fingers means that you fully agree; four fingers means that you agree with most of the decision; and three fingers means you can live with the solution even if you don't like it. By having everyone vote at the same time, no one is able to succumb to group think or peer pressure, and you ensure all voices are heard. Using fist-to-five, you could even start the meeting with a quick poll of each decision. If the team is in agreement about a certain decision, then they don't have to spend time discussing it. They can then focus on discussing decisions that the team doesn't agree on.

Although a constructive debate focused on the issues can be productive and informative, avoid letting the team go around in circles. To do this, you might assign one person to argue for an option and another person to argue against that same option, which ensures that both sides of the debate are represented. Remember that the purpose of the debate is not to "win"; it is to bring issues to light that inform a decision.

For decisions that the team cannot come to consensus on, run short experiments to test possible solutions. Your team might come up with several possible solutions, for example, and then select two or three of them to try out. Alternatively, you could assign people from each side of the issue to work together to design a series of short experiments and then to report back to the group. In many cases, this approach leads to uncovering new options or combining options to arrive at a solution. It also fosters collaboration as members work together to solve the problem rather than focus on making their case and convincing others.

Another technique is to set aside a short time in which meeting attendees can have informal discussion, which is especially important when some (or perhaps all) team members are attending virtually. Be sure to introduce new team members to the team. If the team is large enough, you might have them break out into small groups to talk informally. You could provide a discussion starter, such as asking each person to share something interesting they did over the weekend, or give them a fun team-building exercise, such as trivia questions to answer. Having some unstructured time to get to know each other helps build trust and psychological safety.

Finally, revisit your meeting norms from time to time and ask the team for their feedback. Talk to them about what meeting norms and techniques are working well and what ideas they have for improving meetings. In the spirit of experimentation, you could also try out some new ideas for meetings for a short time and see how they work.

Even though it might feel like a burden to prepare for each meeting, you may find that with this this level of attention, the meetings that you do have are more productive and engaging so you may wind up needing fewer of them.

CREATE KNOWLEDGE NETWORKS

A knowledge network is a group of people who come together to share ideas and expertise on a particular topic. This network can help you sense and interpret what's going on, both inside and outside your organization. While you may be spending considerable time with your immediate team, it's important to sense what's going on in other places. Agile leaders intentionally develop their network to make sure they are getting relevant information when they need it.

To do so, start by thinking about who is already in your network. Remember to think about people you know elsewhere in your organization, such as the budget analyst who helps you complete your unit's budget each year, your former teammate who now works in a different unit, or your previous boss who is now in a higher-level leadership role. Also think about people outside your organization, such as the person you met at the association meeting last month, former college classmates who work in the same field as you (barring any policies or regulations that prohibit you from reaching out to them), or even the author of a work-related blog that you read on a regular basis. Finally, consider who you know that can help you understand different perspectives because of aspects of their background or experience that differ from your own. These differences might come from having varying demographic backgrounds; living in different climates, time zones, or political systems; or working in different sectors or levels in an organization. It's important to include differing perspectives when sensing or interpreting new information or creating a response to try, because research demonstrates that diversity in teams—or in our knowledge network—tends to help us reach more innovation solutions or conclusions. Many of us know people with a range of backgrounds when we take a few minutes to really think about it!

Next, try to connect each person in your network to the type of information or expertise they have. Go back and review the different environmental factors in chapter 1. Ask yourself who you know with expertise in each factor. If you don't know anyone, that's okay! Consider expanding your network to include someone with that expertise. Or maybe one of your teammates has an extensive network in that area that you can draw from. You might not be able to cover every single area by yourself, but by working together with your team, you should be able to cover all of the environmental factors.

Another technique for building your network is to consider ways to meet new people and to maintain relationships both within and outside your organization. To build relationships with those outside your organization, think about joining and becoming involved in professional associations, reaching out to other experts with questions about an article or presentation they gave, or staying in touch with former colleagues. Within your organization, you could offer to give an informational presentation to another department's monthly meeting, participate in a community of practice, or take advantage of organization-wide meetings to meet people from other divisions.

Finally, you can support others as they build their knowledge network. Here are some ideas for you to consider:

- Reward people for learning and applying what they've learned to the job by praising them or recognizing them in a positive way.
- Build learning into your daily work. Have someone research a relevant topic and then present their research at a team meeting, conference, or professional group meeting.
- Set up a community of practice. But beware—simply forming a group will do little to move the needle unless you change the underlying information-sharing norms. We've seen many

communities of practice fizzle out after a few months because their organizational norms say that one should spend time only doing "work," rather than sharing what they know and learning from what their colleagues know.

- Rely on your colleagues to reach out to other experts when you need specific expertise or someone to review a deliverable. Doing so can create a learning opportunity both for you and for the person you are asking help from.
- Facilitate "learning hours," where team members share their expertise or provide a summary of a recent project, experiment, or topic.
- Provide project reviews that inform a manager about technical or functional work being performed while giving quality reviews to the project team.
- Ask a new team member to give a presentation on their previous work or a work-related topic of interest; this is a great way to help newcomers feel that they're valued and have an impact, while ensuring that team members from all backgrounds have a chance to contribute.
- Build and maintain a repository of information and lessons learned.
- Transfer knowledge from employees who are leaving or retiring to your current staff.

Work with your senior leaders to get budget money to invest in these activities, emphasizing that knowledge networks are an investment—not a cost. An expert's investment of a few hours to prepare a presentation that can be delivered multiple times, for example, pays off many times over.

Defining and analyzing your knowledge network can help you make sure that you and others on your team are paying attention to all of the factors that could affect your unit's work. The payoff will come when you identify significant factors early enough to rely on the diversity of ideas and creative solutions that feed into pilots and experiments.

TOOL 5.2: Map Your Knowledge Network

Find twenty minutes of quiet time to refresh your memory about who is already in your network and then use the map below to list them. These could be people you already know or those you could easily reach out to (e.g., the writer of a blog that you read on a regular basis, a professor of a class you took, or an acquaintance you met at a social function). Be sure to cast a wide net: think about academic researchers, former and retired employees, professional colleagues, temporary employees, former interns, professional association members, vendors, suppliers, and more.

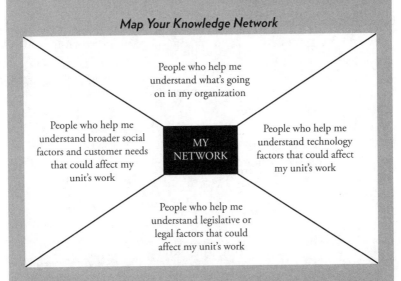

Map Your Knowledge Network

People who help me understand what's going on in my organization

People who help me understand broader social factors and customer needs that could affect my unit's work

MY NETWORK

People who help me understand technology factors that could affect my unit's work

People who help me understand legislative or legal factors that could affect my unit's work

As you review your map, think about the strength of the relationships you have with these people and find a way to indicate this. For example, use plus signs (with stronger relationships getting several plus signs and more distant relationships getting only one) or boxes (drawn darker around stronger relationships and lighter around more distant ones).

Also ask yourself in what areas of expertise you have few (or no) relationships or where you could strengthen your connection with others. How could you find or bolster your relationships with those people? The goal is to build more and stronger relationships with people who have expertise in areas where you need to sense what's going on—while still covering all of the environmental factors so that you avoid blind spots.

An alternative way to fill out the map is to use a mind-mapping tool, which would give you even more flexibility to create new categories. Or, as another alternative, create your own categories on a sheet of paper. Perhaps you want to break out "customer needs" into different products or services. Or maybe you want to add more detail about the individuals in the network you have within your organization; for example, details about people in budgeting versus those in IT versus those in executive leader roles.

Yet another variation would be to use the map as a group exercise. You could ask your team members to write network members on sticky notes; each team member could use a different color sticky note. The combined map would tell you if there are any areas not covered by someone on the team. It would also tell you where there are overlaps in the team's network, in which case, you may want to coordinate who reaches out to certain people so that you're not duplicating efforts. In other cases, it may make sense to have multiple team members in contact with a network person, such as when each team member is talking to the contact about a different topic or when you want some redundancy in your network.

As a final alternative, you could create this map in reverse by listing the people who come to you (and your team members) for information. This would give you an understanding of how your knowledge feeds into others' sensing. Because units in any organization are interrelated, you might benefit from understanding how you fit in to others' knowledge networks. You might find opportunities for sensing and interpreting signals from the environment, collaborating on experiments, or responding to (or preparing for) changes by cross-training employees.

CURATE KNOWLEDGE

An often-overlooked activity that helps promote interpreting information is knowledge curation, which is simply creating an inventory of the information and organizing it meaningfully. We've talked a lot about information sharing and interpreting as well as creating knowledge networks, but whether it's in articles on a certain topic or in relevant takeaways from a discussion with an outside expert it's not enough just to collect all that knowledge. Many teams collect articles, meeting notes, and reports, but if those items stay on individual team members' hard drives (or even paper files), that makes it hard for other team members to access those items (while also breaking an information-sharing norm!). Other times, teams provide access to those items on a shared drive or internal website, which is a great first step to getting information to all team members, but to make it easy for others to know the information exists, you need to take one more step forward and curate it.

To curate knowledge, create an inventory and organize the information into meaningful topics. If you are collecting articles on a specific topic, such as artificial intelligence, you might copy the relevant articles into a shared location that all team members can access. Rather than copy the articles into a location with dozens of articles (or more) on other topics, however, create a subfile or subfolder called "Artificial Intelligence." That way, others who are sensing on this topic could easily find and place articles and other resources into the same folder.

Additionally, you could create a log or inventory of those articles, which could be a simple table that contains the author, date, source, and a one- or two-sentence summary. That summary information could prevent others from having to read through every article to find the information they're looking for. A live (or up-to-date) summary of all past meeting decisions can also help if you have notes that contain decisions and action items from years of recurring meetings, so your teammates don't have to read through it all. (And if you are using a light approach to documenting meetings, that will free up time to create a live summary.)

If you're entering information into a database, be sure to collect information that is actually needed and in a format that is understandable and useful to the recipients. We've seen many instances where considerable resources were used to create a database or other compilation that no one ended up using because the knowledge stored there was either unnecessary or unusable. For example, one organization asked a senior expert to document her expertise before she retired. The expert documented and then filed the information in a way that was useful and meaningful to her—but not to others who needed it after she was gone. This problem could have been avoided by having the senior expert relay the information to her colleagues, such as through a short training session. The colleagues could have then asked questions in order to understand and use the information, documented the knowledge in a format that was useful to them, and then filed the document in a place that they found accessible.

You may need to devote some resources to curating all of the information and knowledge that your team accumulates. Every so often, a team member might need to review and organize the information, which can be a good task for new team members to quickly learn about a relevant topic. Another way to curate information is to assign the role of "knowledge steward" to a team member. Perhaps this role rotates from time to time in order to share the burden and to provide others the opportunity to learn.

Finally, remember not to let knowledge curation take on a life of its own. Yes, you should be keeping information organized and usable for others, and some topics may become less relevant over time and thus may no longer need curation. But you will need to find the right balance between devoting resources to curation and keeping information organized so that it helps the team.

MYTH: TECHNOLOGY WILL SOLVE OUR KNOWLEDGE PROBLEMS

Often, organizations look to technology to solve their knowledge-sharing challenges. This rarely works to solve their knowledge deficits, and teams often end up spending many hours creating and filling a shared drive with unstructured information that ultimately does not get used. As a result, teams can get discouraged about the value of knowledge-sharing efforts, which can hinder agility routines.

That's not to say that creating a shared repository can't be an important step to record and share institutional content; but it alone does not achieve understanding and behavior change. Rather, a technology system must be complemented by the organizational learning approaches described earlier in this chapter. That's because these approaches and tools address the cultural and behavioral issues that are usually the most difficult to change. Wherever implicit and tacit knowledge need to be shared, interactive and iterative forums for sharing that knowledge are needed for personal development and mastery. The shared drive can be a valuable tool in these efforts, but it is not a solution in and of itself.

MYTH: I WON'T HAVE JOB SECURITY IF I SHARE INFORMATION

Many of us are familiar with the coworker who hoards information. Sometimes people do that because they want to feel valued—and they believe that if they share what they know with others, it might diminish their value and they might lose their jobs. But the truth is that one person is unlikely to have all of the information needed in a turbulent situation.

When faced with an employee like this, have a one-on-one conversation with them to explain that information sharing is the norm. Also explain the reasons behind needing to share information. Ask the employee to think about a situation when they needed some information that a coworker declined to share. How did that impact their ability to decide or get something done? You might also probe with questions to understand why the employee doesn't feel psychologically safe enough to share information. You might be able to coach the employee to the point where they feel safe doing so.

Although you might not immediately change the person's mind, you can persist in your efforts to get the team member to adopt new norms. If the employee starts to see that it's really okay to share information and that hoarding information prevents agility, then, ideally, they will start to share information. Pay close attention to any progress in their behavior so that the first time the employee shares something, you will be ready to encourage that behavior. If the employee continues to hold back information, you might need to dig deeper into the psychological safety factors that are still hindering them.

> Feeling Barb's uneasiness with sharing those two events, Blair quickly explains that she isn't interested in playing "Gotcha!" or the blame game; rather, she is focused on making the team as productive as possible. Blair explains that she expects Barb, and any other team member, to talk openly and share work-relevant information—and not to gossip. Using the situation as a learning opportunity, Blair asks Barb, "Did any of your conversations with the team detract from getting work done?" Barb shakes her head, adding, "Of course not! Each conversation only took a few minutes. I didn't interrupt anyone while they were working. I just took advantage of seeing them in the hallway or messaging them at the end of the workday." Blair replies with, "Great—that's exactly what I expect you to do! Don't worry about what other supervisors think. They're free to run their teams how they want. What I want is for you to keep taking the initiative to learn more about what our customers need. As for Vincent, customers who need the standard process aren't going away completely. We need his expertise, and now I know that he will be more comfortable supporting that process."
>
> Blair continues, "What's your next step? Do you have enough information to start testing a new process that would supplement, not replace, how we currently do things?"

"I feel certain that we're going to see more programs with quick-turnaround needs," Barb says, "but I don't know what options are out there. I don't know if we need new software or a different workflow. I can talk to a couple of former team members at different agencies if that's okay." Blair nods. "Yes, please talk to them. And let's talk to a few people who are on the cutting edge— I'll send you contact information for an expert at the Government Contracting Institute (GCI) who I met at last month's conference as well as a university professor who teaches acquisition."

A few days later, Barb updates Blair. "Wow, those conversations with the professor and GCI expert were eye opening! I still need to learn a bit more though. I also will need help applying their insights to our work."

At the next team meeting, Blair asks everyone to create their own knowledge network map. Each team member briefly describes their network, holding their maps up to the screen for others to see. At the end of the meeting, Blair asks them to post their maps on the team's virtual drive.

They discover two key factors that were keeping them from designing a pilot of a more incremental contracting process:

First, only Barry has connections with acquisition software vendors. He started his career in IT and still has some great connections. Blair asks Barry to pull in Barb and Ryan when he starts talking to his contacts, recognizing that Ryan is one of the newest and quietest team members. Blair knows from her one-on-one conversation with Ryan that he'd appreciate being involved.

Second, they discover that they don't really know anyone with policy expertise to help them make sure their new approach would comply with laws and regulations. After brainstorming a bit more, they decide that Blair would reach out to Ms. Barton to explore filling in that part of their knowledge network. Ms. Barton would be able to put Blair in touch with the agency's policy experts.

Blair then starts to plan a few Friday-afternoon knowledge-sharing sessions so that Barry can share what he learns from his network and she can share what she learns from the policy experts. And she might even invite the other supervisor and his team!

Over the next several weeks, Blair continues to devote part of the weekly meeting to knowledge sharing. After talking about information sharing, Ryan and Barry write up a set of eight "information expectation" norms, which the team votes on with a quick fist-to-five. There are a few fours, but that is good enough for the norms to be accepted. And holding up their hands to vote makes yet another virtual meeting a little more bearable.

They also have a couple of quick wins. Ryan uses some information that Vincent shared, which helps Ryan get an urgent request for information completed. Their accomplishment is noticed and greatly appreciated by the program director. And their early successes seem to have made the team even more excited about sharing information.

Getting to this point has taken longer than Blair wanted, and sometimes it feels like they're talking about things that aren't immediately important. However, she realizes that the time they spend in these conversations has the additional benefit of creating stronger relationships among the team. They also are gaining a better understanding of each team member's specific expertise and starting to rely on each other as resources for problem-solving in a way they haven't before. Even quiet members like Ryan are starting to seem more comfortable.

She wants to document what they are learning and proposes a weekly learning log. But the team pushes back hard on that idea. The team feels that they are all involved in the conversations, so spending extra time documenting what they discuss doesn't make sense. And as a result of their stronger connections and the new norm of not hoarding information, if anyone misses the weekly meeting, someone catches them up. The team wants to spend time learning from each other instead of creating lengthy manuals.

Blair agrees with that decision, for now. She knows that it won't take long for the team to realize that they need some amount of documentation. At some point in the near future, someone will likely forget key information previously shared or a new team member will join and need a quick way to get up to speed, and they might see the need. But she also wonders if there is a better way to document the intricacies of their work besides writing it in a manual. "Information is conveyed in so many different ways today—podcasts, videos, online decision aids," she thinks. "Those formats might make knowledge easier to learn." But she is happy with the team's progress for now! So, she decides to apply her current energy to writing a short learning blog for the agency's next all-employee newsletter. She looks forward to sharing her team's recent knowledge-sharing success with the rest of the agency.

SIX

Create Stability

Blair notices that, even with programs that have typical contracting needs, a few issues keep cropping up at predictable times.
Several large programs always seem to need a lot of contracting
work at the beginning of the fiscal year, which requires a lot of
overtime from her team. Even though these programs' needs
are fairly predictable, the team always seems to have a backlog
of work. Another problem that Blair observes is that each team
member takes a slightly different approach, which slows down
the process when they work together on a contract.

  She realizes that the team could benefit from having more
consistent processes and codifying them in a way that they can
easily understand. She just needs to figure out which processes
deserve her attention right now.[1]

Although you can't always control or predict what's going to happen, your team can benefit from stability, as long as you are creating that stability in the right place. Agile organizations enable the
right response at the right time by balancing stability and flexibility. Too much of one or not enough of the other can make the organization less effective. In many cases, too much stability—when it
comes in the form of red tape and unnecessary steps—leads to slow

---

1. Jessica Tierney and Greg Waldrip contributed to this chapter.

responses. Stability can be helpful, however, when it provides the clarity and consistency that supports quick, defensible decisions. Similarly, too much flexibility can result in confusion and inconsistent responses, while the right amount of flexibility lets the organization respond in the right way at the right time. In this chapter, we will explore the stable part of the organization.

MAINTAIN A STABLE ORGANIZATIONAL STRUCTURE

When changes happen quickly, undertaking a major restructuring is unlikely to result in the necessary adjustments, especially if restructuring is the only response. And, in fact, when immediate action is required, a major restructuring is the wrong approach because restructuring cannot be completed quickly. Yet we see many organizations whose sole response to a changing set of events is to restructure themselves. When the pace of change speeds up, traditional organizations often rely on wholesale restructuring, but agile organizations can maintain a quick-response capability by keeping the organizational structure stable, which enables employees to focus on the response. Agile organizations know that revamping the entire organizational structure every time something changes is a losing battle.

Not only are organization-wide restructurings costly, time-consuming, and distracting, but they often do not produce the expected improvements. Instead, they typically pull employees' attention away from changes that are occurring around them, making it likely that they miss important signals. Given how quickly situations can change, the environment may shift many times during the time it takes to restructure! By avoiding unnecessary restructurings, agile organizations help employees sustain their focus on work that is not directly affected by the changes going on around them. This boundary helps everyone ensure timeliness and efficiency.

Although agile organizations reorganize from time to time when major, long-lasting shifts occur, they do not use restructuring as a primary lever for responding to short-term fluctuations. They know that restructuring should be undertaken in only two situations: when you're certain that the change you're responding to is unlikely to change again in the foreseeable future and when a revised structure will support better and faster responses. For example, if your customers change the way they operate, you may benefit by restructuring the parts of the organization that are affected so that employees can better support their customers. Or, if you need to create a new service offering, that may require setting up a dedicated staff and resources as well as a new business unit.

Restructuring doesn't need to be a whole-scale endeavor. It can be as simple as creating new units, combining existing units, separating existing units into smaller components, or removing units that are no longer needed (and reallocating people accordingly). Even if you think that more small-scale restructuring is necessary, however, you may need to garner support for it from other leaders, depending on your leadership role; for example, a first-line supervisor who sees benefits to integrating her team with a peer team would need to start the process by discussing the idea with her manager and the peer team's leader.

You might also consider experimenting to see if your restructuring ideas will produce the results you want: find a way to test a new business model or organizational design, for example. You would likely learn something, which would, in turn, enable you to refine the idea before putting it in place. Let's say you want to combine two units to allow faster responses to changing customer needs and better coordination among employees who support customers. Before making the change, you could ask a few employees from each unit to begin working together. That would give them the chance to document the new process, identify any duplicated efforts, and discover whether any part of the process falls through the cracks. The new processes could then be better defined, leading to a smoother transition.

Although many different organizational structures exist, agile organizations often rely on combinations of structures as a way for each part of the organization to align with its environment. Common organizational structures are functional, divisional, and matrix. A *functional structure* groups people who do similar work, such as work in finance, information technology, acquisition, operations, or human resources. A *divisional structure* groups people according to products or services, type of customers supported, or geographies; each unit contains all of the necessary functions (e.g., information technology or acquisition) to support a service or geography. A *matrix structure* combines elements of functional and divisional structures, grouping people into teams that report to both a functional boss and a divisional boss.

While we don't want to get into a full discussion of the advantages and disadvantages of functional versus divisional versus matrix structures, we do want to emphasize that agile organizations enable both stability and flexibility—which means that, rather than choosing a single type of organizational structure for the entire organization, agile organizations maximize the benefits of each type of structure, using each type where it is needed the most.

Because a functional structure allows processes to be defined, it works well when changes are predictable, understood, and identifiable in advance. The result is often operational efficiency and high levels of productivity. A functional structure also provides a so-called home base that allows employees to develop specific expertise. The stability of a functional home base promotes the career growth of employees who reside in that functional group and allows more experienced employees to mentor and coach those who are less experienced.

A functional structure, however, can be less responsive when unforeseen changes happen, as coordination across the functional units can be time-consuming. Rather than changing the entire organizational structure, then, agile organizations often retain their functional components for predictable changes while incorporating cross-functional teams to accommodate unforeseeable changes. Cross-functional teams bring people together from different functions, allowing them to collaborate more easily to meet customer needs, especially in the face of random events. Cross-functional teams can be formed around specific customers, projects, or programs.

A good example of how cross-functional teams work can be found in hospitals. A hospital system's stable organizational structure helps it respond quickly and effectively when needed. During a medical crisis—such as a pandemic or a mass-casualty event—a hospital doesn't respond by attempting to restructure the entire organization and reallocate employees and resources to the emergency room or intensive care unit. Instead, hospital leaders rely on the organization's structure to determine doctors, nurses, and technicians who can be temporarily reassigned to address the immediate situation.

To be successful, cross-functional teams should have (1) clear goals that align with the organization's strategic goals, (2) members with the right expertise and skills, (3) a leader who approaches leadership with a coaching style, and (4) access to the necessary resources, such as budget and tools. Cross-functional teams also help employees develop specialized knowledge around a customer, project, or program and to broaden their skills across functions.

Cross-functional teams go by many other names, including committees, task forces, tiger teams, rapid-response teams, and so on. They may stand alone or be part of a matrix organization in which employees report to both cross-functional and functional teams. In this way, the agile organization combines stability with a quick-response capability. They gain further flexibility by sending a functional expert on a short-term assignment to help a cross-functional team with a specific problem. Employees can move back and forth between teams depending on the organization's needs and the employees' developmental goals. We'll explore how teams help achieve the right level of response in the next chapter.

Smaller-scale restructuring is another way to respond when needed. For example, it may be faster to reorganize a few units of a few dozen or few hundred people than to reorganize divisions of thousands of people. If you have enough time and are confident that a smaller-scale restructuring will help employees respond to upcoming changes, then go ahead and restructure—or better yet, find a way to pilot your idea with part of the organization first. Also remember that modifying one aspect of the organization means that you will probably need to change other aspects, too, such as processes, roles, decision-making authorities, and the ways different parts of the organization work together.

Finally, if you do restructure, make sure that employees get the support they need to carry out their work in the new structure, or better yet, collaborate on the design of the new structure with the employees who will be affected. Just be sure to explain why a new structure is needed and provide the necessary conditions for the team members to accomplish their work: clear unit goals, defined roles and responsibilities, effective leadership, clear processes, and necessary resources.

TOOL 6.1: When to Restructure the Entire Organization
The table below lists factors to consider as you decide whether to undertake a major restructuring. Circle the scenario in either the left or right column that reflects your organization's situation.

When to Restructure the Entire Organization

Consider Restructuring	Consider Other Ways to Respond
Key factors that affect the entire organization are likely to be stable over the next several years	Key factors that affect the entire organization are likely to shift in the next several years
The shifts that occur will require more coordination among teams	The shifts that occur will not require more coordination among teams
Centralizing certain functions will improve efficiency	Centralizing certain functions will reduce efficiency as well as the ability to respond to unique customer needs
The current structure inhibits a quick response capability	The current structure already supports a quick response capability
Restructuring would support employee development by providing a functional home base	Restructuring would inhibit employee development of functional skills

By engaging in sensing, you will know if and when it is time to restructure. If you are paying attention to the right signals, then you should be able to anticipate a change and undertake a timely restructuring.

IDENTIFY WELL-DEFINED PROCESSES

Another way that agile organizations maintain stability is by figuring out which processes are affected by known factors and can therefore benefit from standardized procedures. Processes that can be defined as a series of steps that should be carried out the same way each time can be normalized. In addition to defining the steps in the process, be sure to clearly define the handoffs at the beginning and end of the process, as that is where things often fall through the cracks and cause problems. For example, IT departments usually have a well-defined process for creating computer system accounts for new employees. When defining these steps, they should indicate what occurs at the beginning of the process—such as an email notification from human resources a few days before the new employee's start date. They should also indicate what happens at the end—such as an email from the IT technician to the new employee's supervisor that says the account has been set up. By explicitly defining every step in the process, including those at the beginning and end, you can ensure all team members are on the same page.

Although well-defined processes are typically used when factors in the environment are not changing in complex ways, changes may still occur that affect a well-defined process. You can prepare for them by creating contingency plans. If unanticipated changes start to occur regularly, then you should reconsider whether the process can continue to be well-defined. The process, or the specific part of the process, affected by unanticipated changes may need to become flexible. For example, when you call a help desk, you usually start off talking to someone who can handle a routine request, such as helping to reset a password or install a software update. If you have a more complicated problem, however, you are usually directed to a different support person who handles less-routine problems. Another example is the payroll process. The steps for making a salary adjustment or changing a tax withholding are known and defined, and these changes generally happen at the same time every year. However, some non-routine, unanticipated changes might be needed throughout the year, such as when a unique new position is created or a law suddenly enacts a temporary change to withholding amounts.

Employees who carry out well-defined processes should, in turn, have roles that are clearly defined. Job aids, "if-then" guidance, and contingency plans can provide structure and definition to employees working in these roles, allowing them to perform the process consistently each time while also helping new-hires learn it quickly. Another way to handle exceptions or unique situations is to have employees seek guidance from more senior employees or supervisors who have relevant expertise. A well-defined process should result in quick, efficient, and consistent products or customer service in most situations, and when a situation warrants a different response, employees should have enough psychological safety to bring in a colleague with more expertise.

Sometimes employees working in a well-defined process can find it helpful to have documentation in the form of job aids, procedures, or templates; however, the time necessary to create complete documentation may not always be warranted or available, such as when employees must respond right away or when a standard response is needed only for a short period. In these cases, here are a few tips to follow for a "just enough" approach to documentation:

- The documentation doesn't need to be pretty; it just needs to be good enough for the purpose at hand.
- The documentation should meet the needs of the audience.
- The documentation should change or be updated as circumstances change; employees working in the process should be able to update the documentation based on what they learn as they carry out their work.
- To prevent silos from forming, employees working in the process should be able to share knowledge often, informally and formally, both with their functional or technical colleagues and with leadership.

Even well-defined processes can be improved. Tools such as business-process mapping, six sigma, and lean six sigma can be used to document existing processes and achieve incremental improvements. Processes can be improved iteratively by identifying possible improvements, trying them out, gathering metrics and stakeholder feedback, and then adjusting.

Steps within a process that do not add value can also be removed. There is a common roadblock to removing steps, however: employees who support those processes usually recognize where non-value-added steps exist, yet they don't have the authority to remove those steps. This roadblock can be addressed by the advice we provided in chapter 4: pushing decisions to the level where the relevant expertise resides will help the organization respond faster and become more efficient. This advice is especially relevant when it comes to refining processes; employees supporting those processes should be given the authority to revise them, including removing unnecessary complexity, as long as they ensure their proposed changes will be effective and defensible. They should be expected to carry out a pilot or experiment, as well, to make sure the changes will not have unintended negative consequences on others, especially on those whose work feeds into or falls downstream of the process.

We've also seen many organizations attempt to improve a process—usually when an employee makes a misstep while carrying it out—by adding steps, reviews, and approvals over time. Unfortunately, this usually makes the process slower and ultimately ineffective. Rather than adding steps when someone makes a misstep, then, the agile organization enables the employee and other team members to learn from the misstep while highlighting part of the process that can, and likely should, be improved.

One way that an increasing number of organizations are speeding up standard processes is to use artificial intelligence (AI) and automation. Using AI allows them to carry out routine work faster while maintaining or even improving consistency and quality. For example, many doctors now use automated systems that incorporate AI to diagnose diseases more accurately than was possible in the past, which helps the doctor select the best treatment approach. As another example, some government agencies that process forms and letters from customers now use AI-enabled systems to route requests to the right person for processing.

But whether you are completely redefining a process, incorporating AI, eliminating steps that don't add value, or adding steps to improve efficiency and standardization, all process changes can be tested using experimentation. Rather than testing out possible redesign solutions in a "live" process, however, it's often best to use an experimentation approach that relies on testing specific parts of a solution in a safe or "offline" manner. Trying out completely new approaches to carrying out a process could be risky and result in highly negative consequences, such as harm to people, delays in service, or dissatisfied customers. For example, it's probably not advisable to put an airplane pilot and passengers in a new type of aircraft that has not first undergone significant safety testing. Rather, the aircraft should be determined as safe through a series of tests. Perhaps, this would start with simulations that show the aircraft can fly at the required altitude and engineering tests to confirm that the materials and structure can withstand takeoffs and landings, eventually leading to test flights under controlled conditions. On the other hand, small or incremental changes to a well-defined process can often be carried out safely, allowing a solution to be refined and confirmed; so it may be perfectly safe to install a new type of seat-back tray in a few airplanes in order to gauge customers' and flight attendants' reactions before installing them across the fleet. But regardless of the testing approach, once a solution is perfected, it can then be integrated into the well-defined process, with job aids updated to reflect new steps.

Finally, if you find that incremental improvements will not yield the results that you need, you may have to consider completely redesigning the process from scratch, which we will explore in more detail in chapter 7.

TOOL 6.2: Where Do You Need Stable Processes?

The factors below can help you figure out which processes (or subprocesses) should be stable and which parts need to be flexible. Because things change rapidly, be sure to periodically reexamine your processes with this tool. You also can rely on your employees, even those performing well-defined processes, to tell you when something has changed—or is about to change—that will affect a well-defined process.

Place an *X* or checkmark along each line below to indicate whether the factors that affect a process (or subprocess) change in straightforward or complex ways.

Where Do You Need Stable Processes?

Name of Process (or Subprocess): _____	
Factors Change in Straightforward Ways	**Factors Change in Complex Ways**
Changes that affect the process don't occur very often. ⟷	Changes that affect the process occur frequently and often.
Only one variable changes at a time. ⟷	Many variables change at once.
Changes are predictable— we know what to look for and when they will happen. ⟷	Changes are unpredictable— we don't know exactly what to look for or when to expect a change to occur.
We can predict what changes will take place. ⟷	We can't accurately predict what changes will take place.
Changes are easy to categorize. ⟷	Changes must be analyzed in order to understand them.
There is one best way to respond to the change. ⟷	There are many possible ways to deal effectively with the change.

More marks toward the left side of the line indicates that a well-defined process may be the best choice, while marks along the right side might tilt decision-making toward a flexible process. You may also want to consider the volume of work handled by the process. High-volume processes, such as routing thousands of forms per year, can be carried out efficiently by a well-defined, and possibly even automated, process. Low-volume processes that occur only a few times per year, such as an annual budget, may require less structure.

TOOL 6.3: Process-Improvement Canvas
When improving a process, it's hard to implement a large number of changes all at once. Too many ideas can be overwhelming and take too long to put into place. That's why we suggest using an iterative approach to improving your well-defined processes. The canvas below shows a variation on a Kanban board; this process-improvement canvas can help you keep track of your team's ideas as they begin to experiment with ways to improve processes.

To use the canvas, identify the particular process you want to address. Then with your team, come to a shared understanding of the problem along with any opportunities for improvement. Ask your team to brainstorm ideas for improving the process; discuss the benefits, risks, and drawbacks of the ideas, then vote on which idea or ideas you want to start trying. Move those ideas into the center column.

Process-Improvement Canvas

What process are we addressing?		

What problem are we trying to solve?		What opportunities do we have for improving the process?

What options do we have for improving the process?	What options are we trying out now?	What options have we already tried?

What are benefits of each option?		What insights or lessons have we learned?

What are the risks or drawbacks of each option?		

After you run an experiment or pilot, document what you learned and what insights you gained. Based on what you learn, you may find that your understanding of the problem evolves and that the possible solutions need to be updated or refined; some solutions may no longer be viable, while new solutions might emerge. As you decide which ideas to try next, proceed until you've achieved the level of performance that you need the process to have.

STAFF STABLE PROCESSES WITH STABLE ROLES

Once you have identified the processes that should be well-defined, you will need to find the right people to carry them out. Agile organizations don't just put anyone into those roles. In addition to making sure that employees have the skills they need for the job (while adhering to legal, human resource, union, and other requirements), agile organizations look for employees who prefer to work in routine and predictable situations.

People tend to self-select into jobs and roles that fit their personalities and interests. So when there's a choice about which role to place an employee in, their ability to deal well with ambiguity is one factor to take into account. Or better yet, ask the employee what her preference is. For example, two engineers with similar skill sets may have different personal preferences about their work; one may prefer the routine of supporting a defined process, while the other may enjoy the variety involved in reengineering processes or defining new ones. Both engineers would look for opportunities to improve processes but would do so in different ways. The engineer supporting the routine process might rely on process-improvement approaches, such as lean six sigma or process mapping, while the other engineer might find that design thinking, use cases, or other innovation approaches are more applicable.

Leaders should demonstrate and communicate that both well-defined and flexible processes and roles provide value to the organization. It's easy for employees to perceive that their work culture prefers one over the other, so leaders should help them understand that both types of processes support organizational agility. Leaders can even turn the tension between the two processes into an ongoing exercise to find the right balance. Of course, the specific roles and number of employees supporting each type of process may change over time. For example, as work becomes more automated, the amount of routine work typically decreases and the amount of non-routine work increases (e.g., handling rare cases, new types of cases, or problems that pop up).

Leaders also need to recognize which employees might not transition easily from a well-defined to a flexible role. Employees who thrive in a predicable routine don't always succeed when every situation requires a different response; conversely, employees who prefer variety and developing creative, yet viable, solutions can be quickly bored by routine work. At the same time, rotating employees within each type of role can promote employee development. Employees in well-defined roles can develop by learning process-improvement tools and techniques as well as specialized functional or technical expertise.

Finally, note that while many organizations have undefined processes that would benefit from more standardization and documentation, the trick is figuring out the right level of detail to include in such documentation. We've seen organizations fail because they provided too much detail and didn't account for a basic level of tacit knowledge. Or they provided too many specifics that would soon be outdated (e.g., when a new software version was released and menu options changed). So be sure that your well-defined processes provide enough clarity without becoming overly specific or detailed.

PROVIDE STABLE NORMS AND EXPECTATIONS

Another way that agile organizations provide stability is through consistent norms. Leaders in an agile organization provide a sense of stability by ensuring that clear, shared norms are accepted and followed. And norms must support the behaviors that are needed. Examples of norms that should not change over time include the following:

- We openly share knowledge as widely as possible.
- We encourage new ideas.
- New ideas can come from anywhere—from any level of the organization and even from outside the organization.
- We learn from experiments and pilots.
- Employee development is an investment.
- Leaders do not have to have all of the answers.

Agile leaders actively manage the organizational culture—which is simply the behaviors and actions that people are expected to carry out—by involving employees in a collaborative discussion to define the norms. As a leader, you can facilitate discussion to identify and define norms that support agility, but the exact wording of these norms should be the employees' own, and the norms should be shared explicitly. Although posting the norms in visible locations, such as in a lunchroom, in a conference room, or on a website is a good way to make them explicit, you will need to do more to get employees to follow them. Some employees will instantly try out the new norms to see if it's really okay to follow them, while others will wait to see what happens to those who are early adopters.

To encourage adoption, you must find positive examples of people displaying the norms and be genuine when you highlight those positive examples. Think back to chapter 2 and the skills you developed in giving specific, positive feedback. When you see someone acting in accordance with a norm, point it out to reinforce that the person did the right thing. This might be a simple "You did a great job listening to your coworkers' idea" or a shout-out in an email or newsletter. Keep in mind that praise should be meaningful to the employee you're giving it to. In other words, not everyone relishes public recognition, so a more personal "thank you" may be better for some. You may need a keen eye to spot these behaviors at first but will probably find them easier to spot as time goes on and the norms begin to take hold.

Another way to catch someone doing the right thing is to ask employees to share their own examples of adhering to the norms. Some organizations hold daily or weekly status meetings, which are great opportunities to allocate five minutes for employees to share examples of their own or teammates' actions that demonstrate desirable behaviors. At first, sharing positive examples might seem like bragging, so make sure to draw a connection between the examples and team norms. This practice does not have to be time-consuming or permanent either. Use it when your team is working on adopting a new norm and retire it when you've implemented the changes that you or your team desired.

Finally, explain your actions and decisions in reference to the norms. It's not always obvious to employees how you arrived at a course of action or decision; some explanation of your rationale and thought process can help demonstrate your commitment. You might explain that a certain decision was made by testing out two options, for example. Or you might describe the process you went through to make the decision, explaining your decision-making approach. If you are a new leader, ask other leaders to share the organization's norms if necessary. They will likely want to gain your buy-in. Communicate your acceptance of and intention to keep those norms to engender trust while maintaining the sense of psychological safety in the organization.

MYTH: WE CAN RESPOND TO FREQUENT CHANGES BY RESTRUCTURING

We've seen many organizations use restructuring as the primary mechanism for responding to change. When we talk with employees whose organization is undergoing a restructuring initiative, we often hear that only the "boxes and lines" on the organization chart will change, despite significant resources allocated to the effort. Employees frequently also describe a range of less-than-desirable results from restructuring, including processes that remain unchanged, roles that become more unclear, and an increased mistrust of leaders who don't adequately communicate the reasons behind the restructuring. To employees facing turbulent, complex changes, having to focus on figuring out a new structure takes time that could otherwise be devoted to agility routines. In short, employees often perceive that restructuring will not address the changes that the organization is facing.

The truth is that when situations change rapidly and in complex ways, establishing teams is a much more effective way to deal with those changes than restructuring. We will talk more about how you might leverage small teams to respond to rapid, complex change in the next chapter. For now, let's just say that keeping the organizational structure stable can help keep everyone focused on responding.

Blair decides to chat with Vincent. She explains, "Our standard contracting process isn't going anywhere. The work that Barb is leading—to explore ideas for a more incremental approach—will never completely replace what we usually do. Instead, we may have two approaches operating at the same time. Let's talk more about why our standard approach still isn't always getting us the results we want. I'd like you to lead an effort to update the process guide."

Vincent expresses relief that Blair isn't throwing out a perfectly good process. He replies, "Well, the process guide does need some improvement. Some parts of it are incomplete; other parts aren't written down. And another part of the problem might be that the process described in the guide is just inefficient."

She suggests that he get help from a couple team members and ask them to use their network—people on their team, on other teams, and in the programs—to come up with ideas for improving the guide. She also gives him the email address of a process-improvement specialist in the western division.

A week later, Barry asks if they need to restructure the division so that they can meet the new requests from programs.

"No, not right now," Blair says, "but it might be a possibility in the future, depending on what Barb learns about the programs' needs. First, we need to focus on designing a more responsive process that improves our efficiency for standard contracts. If we think that the programs will continue to need an incremental process, then we can decide if we need to change our structure. I don't want to reorganize if the programs' quick-turnaround needs won't continue."

"Will we all be required to learn the new process?" Vincent asks.

"Of course not," Blair responds. "I want you all to be learning new things. But I won't force you to learn; what you learn is really up to you. And we need your expertise on the standard process, Vincent."

Relieved, Vincent starts to see a new role for himself, one in which he can rely on all of his years of experience to finally work out the kinks in the standard process. He also realizes that taking out the quick-turnaround work will speed up the processing for standard contracts. He tells Blair, "Barb and I will need to find a way to route incoming requests into the right process. If we can do that, then it should be possible to update the steps in the process guide, get everyone on the same page, and quickly train new team members."

Blair nods approvingly. "That's a great idea! I know you have a lot of knowledge in your head. The team would really benefit from documenting all of that knowledge so that they can learn from you."

Blair starts to feel that the tension between the "old" and "new" way of doing things may be starting to dissipate. She's heard some of the more experienced team members complain that newer team members ignore the process guide, while newer employees say the more tenured team members are stuck in their ways. Blair's message that both the old and new ways are necessary—reinforced by her efforts to put people into roles that support each—might be starting to sink in. Blair is confident that getting everyone working on the same page with the process guide will improve the team's efficiency in carrying out routine work.

SEVEN

Create Flexibility

A few months have passed since Blair asked the team to update the process guide. Vincent, along with a few others, reworked the guide, renaming it the playbook. Its new name reflects that it is now a more user-friendly resource, with helpful checklists and visual aids organized in a way that supports the team, rather than a recitation of policy and rules. Vincent even led a couple of informational sessions to bring the team up to speed. Blair starts to notice concrete improvements in how quickly they now process standard contracts. Turnaround time has gone down quite a bit, and they're reducing the backlog of work while building close relationships with the program managers.

As Blair preps for her regularly scheduled one-on-one check-in with Ms. Barton, she reflects on the progress she's seen in establishing a more stable process for routine contracts. She also wants to focus her attention on the new, more flexible contracting approach that her team has just started to see a need for. She especially would like to encourage them to learn and experiment with ways to be responsive to the programs. Figuring out where to be more rigid and where to be more flexible is a challenge Blair decides to raise with Ms. Barton.[1]

---

1. Awais Sheikh contributed to this chapter.

Now let's turn our attention to how to embed flexibility. One way to provide this flexibility is by keeping the organization's structure stable, as discussed in chapter 6, and then supplementing it with small teams that quickly test possible solutions using experiments and pilots. Rapid experiments help diagnose the problem, identify which solutions are likely to work, and quickly refine solutions. Pilots are small-scale implementations of solutions used to refine and improve the solution before rolling it out on a larger scale. Rapid experiments and pilots can also be used to find new opportunities to improve how work is carried out.

RESPOND WITH TEAMS

Agile organizations deploy a wide range of teams to respond to crises or explore emerging trends or pressing issues. Sometimes, teams are short-term or quick-response; other times they may endure. They go by various names: task forces, crisis teams, tiger teams, and rapid-response teams. Some teams may form on their own, while others may form at the direction of a leader. Employees who have already come together, whether virtually or in person, to sense and interpret what a change means might want to continue to explore the change by considering responses. In agile organizations, not only do leaders request that teams be formed to address specific problems, but collaborative norms permit employees to decide if and when they want to get involved in teams to address the swirl of change.

Creating a formal, temporary team brings some advantages—the team can request resources that it needs to test and experiment with possible solutions. Higher-level leaders, who provide access to resources the team may need, also provide top cover for the team, authorizing them to continue their activities. With an emphasis on quick, inexpensive experiments, temporary teams often do not require significant funding; in fact, resources are conserved when solutions are found sooner through low-cost experiments.

Of course, those in positions of formal authority may also serve on temporary teams, bringing their technical or functional expertise to bear on the problem as well as their knowledge about where to find other experts and resources across the organization. Employees can decide if and when to join a temporary team as well; as the team interprets signals that it is picking up on through sensing, its understanding of the problem may change, resulting in a need for new or different expertise. So temporary teams are expected to form, reform, and disband appropriately.

Agile organizations rely on temporary teams to respond both reactively and proactively. Not every change that affects the organization will be noticed before it happens. Sometimes, the organization is affected by something that comes out of the blue, requiring you to scramble to find a response; however, doing a good job staying on top of what's about to change or might change, through sensing routines, allows the organization to anticipate change and to try out different responses before they are needed.

When a team is faced with a rapidly evolving situation, they'll sometimes find that the situation has shifted again, even before a response was found to address the original problem. In this case, the team may need to speed up its experimental cycle. As previously mentioned, experiments can be done quickly and inexpensively by testing out essential parts of a solution rather than a full-blown version, so this may be a technique that the team needs to try. Another way to deal with rapidly changing situations is to pull in new team members with different expertise. The team shouldn't be locked into its current members—it may need to switch them up.

Changes that are expected to last longer can be addressed by using more permanent project teams or task forces. Employees can be matrixed out to such teams, and long-term team assignments can help employees gain specialized knowledge about a specific customer or service offering.

Another type of team that can be created to manage the swirl of change is the on-call team, which springs into action on demand. Even though it's impossible to predict every exact situation, you can often predict that something will happen at some point. In that case, your on-call people can jump in; until then, they can perform their regular jobs.

No matter the type, teams provide a way to bring together employees from across the organization, helping ensure the right skill sets are brought to bear. Given the collaborative nature of agile organizations, employees are permitted—and even encouraged—to form teams spontaneously and to change team membership and disband when they see fit. Because employees are expected to share information about changes and to work together to figure out what those changes might mean for the organization, self-forming teams are a natural result. They may form to share signals that people are sensing, discuss how processes might be affected, then come up with ideas for quick, iterative experiments that could lead to a solution.

Whether self-forming or leader-directed, however, it is important to keep teams small; research shows that small, even two- or three-person teams, can provide powerful results. In small teams, it is easy to keep everyone up to date and on the same page, assuming that the team has the right skill sets.

Also keep in mind that, although some teams form on their own, they may require resources as well as some degree of oversight and support from leaders, if only as part of information sharing. Leaders can reinforce teams in many ways. They can ensure that norms support sensing, interpreting, and responding routines. They can ensure psychological safety—the sense that it's okay for people to try possible solutions, learn from experiments, and share what they learn as they go along. Leaders can help ensure that budgets include enough resources to enable experimentation. And they can provide top cover and help keep their own leaders, whom they report to, informed of the team's progress.

INCORPORATE INNOVATION TECHNIQUES TO SOLVE PROBLEMS

Building teams is an important first step toward solving a problem. So teams should start by generating ideas to address the problems. New and complex problems require fresh thinking to develop new solutions or adapt them from another context. Luckily for leaders, this process need not be mysterious or reserved for a select few. You're probably familiar with some techniques for encouraging divergent thinking, such as brainstorming or identifying unintended consequences. Another divergent thinking technique is *design thinking*, a human-centered approach to generating and testing novel ideas that has demonstrated success in helping cross-functional teams generate, select, and prototype ideas to solve complex problems.

Design thinking begins with the team immersing itself in the problem context, usually by empathizing with the stakeholders that the team is designing solutions for. An example of this is exploring a stakeholder's experience through a journey map, which is a visual way of showing the stakeholder's experience. The journey map captures stakeholders' pain points and opportunities at various points during that experience. Once the team has explored the problem space, it defines alternative problem frames to decompose the complex challenge into a more manageable set of problem areas that the team can try to influence.

The different problem frames lend themselves to structured brainstorming sessions to identify a large number of ideas. While the term *brainstorming* has been overused and often signifies people being put on the spot to share ideas that are then judged, design thinking emphasizes a series of rules and methods for brainstorming that engages the full team in a less threatening manner. Examples of these rules and methods are visualizing the process, such as by using sticky notes or pictures, and deferring judgment for others' initial ideas, instead focusing on quantity. After the team has identified a large number of ideas, it selects which ideas to explore. Teams are encouraged to think of individual ideas as puzzle pieces or blocks that can be combined into different configurations, as some of the best ideas are often the combination of two or more disparate ideas.

Once the team has identified a handful of alternative ideas to explore, it needs to find a way to surface and test the assumptions behind those ideas. This is where experimentation and piloting come into play.

CONDUCT RAPID EXPERIMENTS AND PILOTS

Leaders are often challenged with implementing innovative solutions in uncertain environments given a number of variables that they must account for. *Assumptions* is another term for these variables.

Think of assumptions as a series of constraints that you must operate within. As agile leaders, however, you can lean into these assumptions to create flexibility.

That flexibility comes from your signals to your teams to conduct rapid experiments and pilots and to explore the assumptions inherent within current and potential problems. Experimentation and pilots allow your teams to iteratively uncover the best solution before the change or problem affects your organization.

Experimentation entails designing and executing a series of controlled investigations to systematically test the essential assumptions behind possible solutions. By definition, an experiment will not require a complete solution. Instead, you will want to design an experiment that enables maximum learning with the least amount of effort. With some creativity and planning, a team can often find quick, safe, cost-effective ways to test whether a solution will work. Before you try to implement an expensive, complex automated solution, for example, you can test the process manually to see whether the capability produces the desired outcomes. Because automation often impacts multiple processes and requires workflows to be redesigned, we suggest that you test out the redesigned process before implementing automation; this will help your team understand how the automation works as well as identify unanticipated effects.

Another approach to experimentation is to use a control group as a baseline against which you can compare possible solutions. Rather than roll out a solution across the organization, try testing it with a small group—perhaps a project team, office, or region. Then refine the solution with that group before rolling it out to the next one. For example, if a process needs to change as a result of a new policy or technology, experiment with two or three ways of modifying the process. Then try each option with a few simple cases. Review the results together, refine the options, and try again with slightly more complex cases. Keep experimenting, learning, and refining until the team settles on a solution.

Piloting means conducting a practice or trial run of a solution with the goal of learning what aspects of the solution work well and what aspects don't. In response to this learning, changes and improvements to the solution can be made, and another pilot can be conducted to test out the refined solution. The cycle of pilot, refine, repilot should continue until the final version is agreed upon. At this point, you and your team can roll out the solution. There's no correct or ideal number of pilots to conduct before deciding to make the solution final, and while some of the final versions may become well-defined processes (or integrated into well-defined processes), other versions may be intentionally flexible.

Let's say you want to implement a mentoring program for new team members. You could start with a small pilot where you train two or three mentors and have them start to work with the new team members. Ask the mentors and new employees for feedback and ideas for improving the program. They might have ideas for how to improve the program itself, such as implementing a process for signing up to be a mentor or for assigning mentors to new employees. They also might have ideas for how to improve mentoring, such as ways that mentors can build rapport with new employees. Incorporate one or two of these ideas into a slightly more expanded pilot, continuing to iterate until a full-scale mentoring program is underway. At that point, you know that the program is working well, and you've developed it with an initial minimal investment.

Experimentation and piloting help you work efficiently because you're not investing large amounts of resources up front for a program or solution that turns out not to work perfectly. In the past, some organizational leaders tried to solve problems or put programs into place all at once, often requiring large multiyear investments. That approach worked well when situations changed slowly and when those leaders had near-perfect knowledge about the organization. However, most organizational changes now should be addressed iteratively because no one person has enough of a grasp of an issue to solve it. For example, organizations can develop clear organizational policies by implementing a few straightforward rules, seeing how they influence employees' work and decisions, and then adjusting the policy statements appropriately.

TOOL 7.1: Map Your Assumptions

You might want to use an assumption map like the one below to identify the topics for your experiments or pilots. The first step is for your team to surface all of the assumptions that would need to be true for an idea to be successful in solving a problem. Humans tend to make three types of assumptions:

- Stakeholder-needs assumptions: We assume that we know our stakeholders' (or customers') needs.
- Solution-fit assumptions: We assume that our proposed solutions will adequately address our problems or meet our stakeholders' needs.
- Solution-feasibility assumptions: We assume our solutions are feasible to develop and sustain.

When our solutions don't work, we often find out after the fact that one of our assumptions was incorrect. So by recognizing our assumptions early, we can modify our solution to make sure it works.

When faced with a problem, ask your team to identify assumptions they are making. You might ask each team member to spend five to ten minutes listing assumptions; then call on each team member to share one assumption at a time, until everyone has shared what they think. You could also have your team identify assumptions as a group; they could write assumptions on sticky notes, for example, and then post them on a wall or flip chart so that they are visible to the group.

List Your Assumptions

Type of Assumption	Our Assumptions
Stakeholder-Need Assumptions: What do we think our stakeholders really need?	
Solution-Fit Assumptions: How will this solution address the problem or need?	
Solution-Feasibility Assumptions: How will we develop and sustain the solution?	

Once the team has identified assumptions, they can map the assumptions onto a matrix like the one shown below. The *x* axis of the matrix is the level of certainty around the assumption; assumptions that you are highly certain are true would go toward the right side, and assumptions that you are not certain are true would go toward the left side. The *y* axis of the matrix is the importance of the assumption to the viability of the solution. Assumptions that must be true for a solution to work would go on the top half of the matrix, while those that don't need to be true for a solution to work would go on the bottom half.

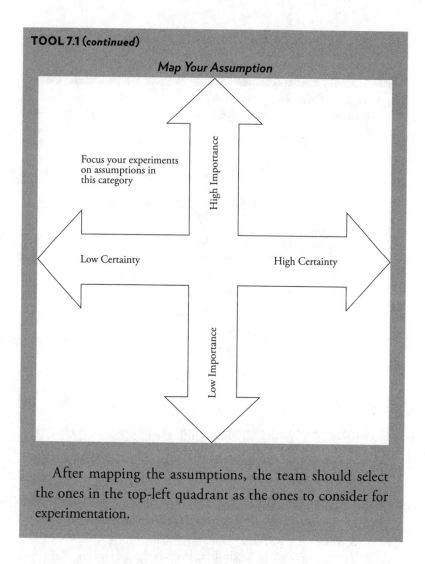

Map Your Assumption

Focus your experiments on assumptions in this category

High Importance

Low Certainty

High Certainty

Low Importance

After mapping the assumptions, the team should select the ones in the top-left quadrant as the ones to consider for experimentation.

IDENTIFY FLEXIBLE PROCESSES

Sometimes it is not possible to specify a detailed series of steps or create contingency plans. Agile organizations respond to such situations by identifying processes that need to be flexible. Flexible processes are necessary when the situation drives how the work is carried out and when that situation is ever-changing in complex and unforeseen ways. In some cases, you might not be able to predict when the situation will change, but once it does, you can be prepared by having an alternate approach. In other cases, complex factors might interact in new ways, resulting in one-time solutions. For example, redesigning an organization's financial systems depends on many factors, including the organization's finance needs, the accounting and budgeting software and systems that employees rely on, information-security details, and finance regulations. Although a solution architect might follow the same general steps each time she designs a new financial infrastructure (e.g., review the current infrastructure, identify future needs, and design the new architecture), the architect also relies on expertise and experience to create a final solution that's specific to the organization's requirements.

Yet another part of your role as a leader in an agile organization is to contribute to this norm of making intentional decisions about which processes are well-defined and which are flexible. To do so, you can get input from other knowledgeable people. You can make sure that flexibility is not misapplied or used as an excuse for not taking the time to define and document processes that need to be stable. You can also help employees distinguish between situations requiring well-documented or flexible approaches, emphasizing that neither is inherently right or wrong but that both approaches serve customers equally well in specific contexts. For example, people working in different geographical locations or serving customers with slightly different needs may need to customize processes according to stakeholder needs, the physical layout of their offices, location-specific policies and regulations, or other unique circumstances.

To distinguish (or help your team distinguish) whether a situation might warrant more flexibility, keep in mind that well-defined processes allow your team to get work done quickly and efficiently because the steps are clear. It's okay to allow for differentiation from the steps, of course, but consider carefully before customizing a well-defined process; you don't want people reinventing the wheel so that it detracts from focusing on work and wastes resources. Also know that one-off processes make it more difficult to train, cross-train, and rotate employees across units as well as to improve processes. That said, there are situations (as mentioned earlier in this section) where flexibility is not only warranted but necessary.

Finally, after deciding which processes (or parts of processes) are stable and which are flexible, organizations should specify these and communicate them with those actually carrying out the processes. And remember that all processes—both flexible and well-defined— should be periodically reviewed in order to identify where improvements might be made, either through refining steps, making parts of a process more stable or flexible, or even eliminating processes that are unnecessary or add little value.

STAFF FLEXIBLE PROCESSES WITH FLEXIBLE ROLES

When work must be carried out in a different way each time or when it's impossible to define work as a series of distinct steps, you will need to rely on your expertise and experience, along with that of your teammates, to find the best flexible approach. For example, organizations with complex computer systems running multiple applications may find it difficult, if not impossible, to create step-by-step plans that will cover every possible set of problems, so they must rely on computer-systems experts to diagnose and solve non-routine problems.

In some cases, well-defined processes can be combined with flexible processes. For instance, a computer specialist might analyze a system crash by drawing on her expertise to decide which tests to run or system logs to review to pinpoint the cause. Upon finding out that the system crash was caused by a specific software application, she might then use a job aid, perhaps a reference manual provided by the software vendor, to walk through the specific steps her team should follow to bring the software back online.

Flexible processes are best staffed with employees who thrive on ambiguity. These processes may also be staffed with a mix of technical or functional experts with some degree of creativity who can draw on their expertise to quickly find and test possible solutions. Role descriptions for employees supporting flexible processes should focus on responsibilities and broad outcomes rather than on compliance with defined steps or actions. Such flexible role descriptions allow employees the latitude they need to respond to the wide range of situations they may encounter. Note, however, that employees supporting flexible processes will likely also perform tasks that intersect with well-defined processes by helping to identify and test improvements to those processes.

MYTH: WE HAVE TO BE A WELL-FUNCTIONING ORGANIZATION BEFORE WE CAN BE FLEXIBLE

We often hear employees and leaders say that they need lots of standardization before they can begin incorporating agility. Not so. These organizations are usually not getting the results they want and are incorrectly assuming that they need to define processes before enacting changes to them. The range of obstacles to flexibility cited by these organizations include the following:

- We need a few more months (or years) to define and standardize how we do things.
- If only things would stop changing for a while, we would have time to get everyone on the same page.
- We are short-staffed or underfunded right now—we hope to hire more employees or get more funding next fiscal year.
- We just need people to work a few more hours each day to get everyone on the same page, but they are already overworked and responding to urgent situations.
- We formed a task force to document our processes, but the task force was overtaken by events beyond their control; task force members lost focus when they were pulled off to fight fires (i.e., deal with more pressing issues).

You may think you don't need to prepare your organization to handle all of the demands and evolving situations that you will, in fact, face. We recognize that you are doing your best and have good intentions. And we know it is not easy to get an organization to adopt agility principles while having to carry out work in the face of rapid change—and usually with an understaffed and underfunded organization. However, it's unlikely that your environment will ever get back to a state of stability and certainty, especially if you don't consider ways to achieve the right balance between stability and flexibility. That isn't necessarily an easy thing to do, but the truth is you probably don't have a choice due to the constant state of flux confronting us all right now—that state where what needs to be stable today may need to be flexible tomorrow. Becoming more agile means finding a new way to approach work, starting with acknowledging that some processes may need to be flexible while others may benefit from being well-defined.

MYTH: DEVELOPING INNOVATIVE IDEAS IS A MYSTERIOUS PROCESS

Sometimes people see innovation as something that only a few creative individuals can carry out. Other times, people think that you have to have "innovation" in your job title to come up with new ideas. The truth is that all individuals and organizations can both learn and practice innovative behaviors, helping them to identify and explore new ideas. Design thinking and lean startup are examples of repeatable, proven approaches that can be used to explore unmet customer needs and ideas to meet those needs. Leaders who recognize that many different innovation techniques exist and can be used by anyone will help further innovation; using these innovation techniques helps employees become familiar with the approaches and unlock their creative ideas. Perhaps more importantly, using innovation techniques regularly allows employees to come up with unique ideas that can be tested and put into practice—and this results in the "I'm not creative" mindset retreating with visible, tangible impact.

A related misconception is that innovation can be carried out by simply trying a bunch of ideas and then seeing what works. Some organizations use terms like *pilots* and *prototypes* to refer to different ways of approaching a problem, but many times, they don't invest time to define the problem first. Instead, they jump into identifying possible solutions. They view the pilot or prototype as a way to try out multiple ideas at the same time without defining what success really looks like.

To prevent this from happening, we recommend that you and your organization take a structured approach to experimentation by defining the success criteria ahead of time and then identifying and testing one idea at a time, in short iterative cycles. Knowing what success looks like will help you assess the results at the end of the experiment. And if you are a leader who is trying to promote organizational agility, we encourage you to not be afraid that an experiment will not meet the stated success criteria—whatever happens will provide useful feedback and allow you to refine the ideas and eventually find a solution that works.

Blair calls in to her meeting with Ms. Barton. Among other updates, Blair lets Ms. Barton know that the team is creating a separate, more flexible process to use for programs that need smaller, more frequent contracts. Ms. Barton seems to appreciate the update, saying, "Let me know if I can introduce you to any contracting experts in the other divisions."

With Vincent and his team working on documenting the standard process, Blair asks Hari and two other team members whose programs are in a lull to help out another division experiencing the typical October surge of contracts. "Not only will this help out the other division, but it will give Hari and the others a great opportunity to learn about contracting for products as opposed to our team's focus on services," Blair explains at the weekly meeting. "What they learn might come in handy and continue to build our relationships within the agency's contracting community."

In the interim, two additional teams formed on their own. Barb didn't have time to look into new acquisition tools, so Hank and Kyle volunteered to help. And when Maya attended Blair's learning hour on changing laws and policies, her eyes lit up, and she offered to get involved; it turns out that Maya's minor in college was public policy.

It took a couple of months for Hank and Kyle to narrow down the acquisition tools to a manageable number, especially given their current workloads. But they managed to fit in their research along with a few calls to acquisition experts inside and outside their agency. After some short initial conversations with the tool vendors, Hank arranged for a few vendors to provide tool demos for the entire team. Several team members, including Vincent, posed some very insightful questions that helped the team understand which tools would work best. And by involving everyone, the team seemed to take ownership in the decision, while Blair started talking to Ms. Barton about how to fund the new tool. Blair told Ms. Barton that it was Kyle who realized that the current system might cost them less when they start transitioning quick-turnaround work to the new tool, which would free up most of the funding they needed to buy it.

Blair asks Hank and Kyle to start thinking about how to experiment with a new process and run a series of pilots with the new tool. To help figure out what to pilot, Blair puts them in touch with an expert in the agency's innovation center. The expert helps them run a design-thinking workshop where acquisition team members across the agency try to reimagine what the process might look like as well as identify certain assumptions that they'd been making. The assumptions, along with a vision of a smoothly running, yet flexible process, help Hank and Kyle plan a series of experiments. Hank is able to get trial versions of a couple of tools so that they can experiment with an outline of a possible new process.

Kyle suggests, "Could you pull up a set of previous quick-turnaround contracts, strip out sensitive information, then practice routing them through the new tools? We could start with three or four test cases. I'm sure we'd learn a lot as we went, and we could even start to pull in other team members to help. That would give them a chance to learn the new tools and be in a better position to decide which one works best."

"That's a great idea!" Blair responds. "Several team members have been asking for a chance to brush up on their technical skills. Just last week, Barb mentioned that her friends at other agencies are already familiar with some of these tools, and she doesn't want to be left behind."

Hank adds, "Once we learn which tool works best, we can pilot the process with some easy contracts. Kyle and I can then work out the details of the process and expand the pilot to a few more team members and contracts. I'm sure they'll have some good insights into where we need to define clear steps and where we need to give them flexibility to address the program's unique needs. And some of these tools are using artificial intelligence that learn as they go along; if we used those tools, we would need to pull in some past cases anyhow."

Blair agrees, thinking, "This is working well. In the past, the decision about which tool to buy would have come from several levels up. The team would have resisted because they would have thought, correctly so, that those decision-makers are too far removed from the day-to-day contracting work to pick the right tool. Keeping Ms. Barton in the loop, though, has paid off, and she's been really supportive. And she seems to appreciate not having to spend her time making this decision."

However, at her next check-in with Ms. Barton, Blair learns that Mrs. Banks has expressed concern about Blair's team taking so much time to run experiments. Blair and Ms. Barton discuss how to address this concern, focusing on the productivity improvements that they have already seen.

Ms. Barton notes, "It will be hard for Mrs. Banks to deny that you're making progress when she sees how the team is turning around standard contracts much faster now."

Blair adds, "I expect that we will continue to improve, especially when we tackle the incremental contracts we're seeing so much of. And we think our quality will go up. By drafting a contract right the first time, we reduce our rework time and are less of a burden on the programs. Another way to explain why we're changing the way we work is to share all of the factors that impact our work—I know you remember back when I first took the job, how we documented all of the changes going on. That might help her see that we can't keep doing work the same way if everything around us keeps changing."

A few weeks later, Hank updates Blair on the experiments: "When we explained the new process, we hadn't accounted for needing to route work requests into the right workflow—either the typical or new process. When we started the experiments, we realized that people were getting confused about which workflow to use. We had to spend time creating a routing process, but it's a good thing we caught that early. We hadn't even thought about that until we started running a test! It was one of the testers who came up with a really creative, yet effective, way to route the work into the right workflow."

Blair realizes that pilots and experiments do take time and mental energy but will lead to the results that her team ultimately needs. Now that the team has started to implement the guide-lines in the playbook, Blair is already seeing that they will need fewer team members working on routine work; this means that more of the team will be available to handle the non-routine work.

Ms. Barton sends Blair a quick email to fill her in on the meet-ing with Mrs. Banks, saying that it went well and that the hard data on their productivity was hard to argue with. That said, Mrs. Banks was still not completely convinced.

Blair jots down a quick reminder for her next check-in with Ms. Barton—they'll need to figure out how to get Mrs. Banks on board at some point. In addition, Blair begins to realize that her team's progress can only go so far without other parts of the organization being on board too. So far, her team had been the only one in the organization to become more agile in response to the programs' becoming more agile. To help other parts of the organization—finance, accounting, human resource manage-ment, and IT—to become more agile will require a higher-level leader to start them down that path.

EIGHT

Encourage the Routines

While the team is making good progress on both stable and flexible processes, Blair has a bit of extra time to reflect on what is working well and where she should encourage the team to focus next. They have developed a good understanding of all the factors that affect their work, but Blair thinks they are still a little reactive. She has started to detect a little bit of pushback from Barb and Vincent. In particular, Barb has made a few comments that suggest she thinks the sensing and responding routines could be a waste of time. Blair decides to strengthen the case for agility by focusing on how well the team has developed their skills and by showing them how their efforts have started to pay off. She decides it's time to revisit the idea of sensing and responding now that the team is a bit more familiar with those ideas.

By this point, we hope that you've started to make significant inroads with psychological safety. You also may have started to use some of the levers—pushing decisions to the right level, promoting learning, adapting your leadership actions, and identifying processes and roles that need to be stable or flexible. Remember, however, that you won't be able to make as much progress as you want with the levers if there is not sufficient psychological safety. So if you are not seeing progress, be sure to revisit chapter 2 on psychological safety.

Now let's circle back to the environment and talk about how you can encourage sensing, interpreting, and responding routines. We use the term *routines* to convey that these are habits or recurring behaviors. When the environment is turbulent, it takes focus, energy, and force of habit to stay on top of changes—this is where sensing comes in. The situation has to be constantly monitored to know when something has changed or even if it hasn't. When new information comes in, it may not always be obvious what, if anything, this input means for the organization, its mission, and its work. Interpreting now comes into the picture—people have to work together to make sense of the information and decide whether the organization needs to do something about it. A response may need to occur right away or one may need to be prepared for the future.

GET EVERYONE INVOLVED IN THE ROUTINES

First, set a new norm that says everyone in the organization must get involved in the routines in some way. Because different people have different skill sets, interests, and perspectives, not everyone will or should get involved in sensing the same information or in figuring out a response to every change. Let your team know that you expect them to get involved but leave it up to them exactly how they make that happen.

You might provide ideas to get them started. Make sure they know how much time they are expected to spend on sensing and interpreting when it is not directly related to their job. Sometimes, people are already doing some sort of sensing and interpreting, and even responding, as part of their daily duties. Giving them concrete examples of the ways they are carrying out these norms will help it sink in that they are already engaging in the routines. Another way to help make these new behaviors stick is to hold daily five-minute check-ins with your team, which will give them a chance to quickly ask questions and get feedback and show that you're committed to supporting them.

TOOL 8.1: Where Can We Be More Proactive?

When you started this journey, we asked you to start looking at all of the factors currently influencing your organization. Now that you've made progress, let's revisit those factors and dig a bit deeper by looking at which ones have affected your organization in the past, which ones are affecting your organization now, and which ones might affect your organization in the future. To get started, revisit the factors—trends, patterns, problems, and opportunities—that you identified in chapter 1, adding anything new that you think of. Then use these factors to fill out the table below. You might start by filling out the table yourself and then asking others to add their input. Or you might use it as an exercise during a team-planning meeting, having team members write factors on sticky notes and then posting them on the wall or on flip-chart paper.

In the "Past" column, identify problems that caught you by surprise as well as those you spotted in advance and had time to prepare for. You could also think of opportunities that you were able to take advantage of. As you identify these factors, you might also jot down what you learned and how the organization adapted—or, in hindsight, how it could have adapted. Then finally, you might ask what you can do to sense for these factors so that they don't take you by surprise again.

In the "Present" column, list factors that you are currently aware of, including problems and opportunities that the organization is facing immediately or will face in the near future. Ask yourself whether you became aware of these factors in enough time to prepare a response. If not, what sensing could have occurred to give you more advance notice?

In the "Future" column, list factors that you know will or could affect the organization. As you review these future factors, ask yourself which ones you should start figuring out a response for now and which ones warrant monitoring. Are there groups of factors that could be monitored together? Or are there groups of factors that you could simultaneously prepare a response for?

Where Can We Be More Proactive?

	Past	Present	Future
Legislative or Legal Factors			
Social Factors			
Technology Factors			
Customer Factors			
Natural Disasters or Events			
Factors from within Your Organization			

You should find it encouraging when others identify factors that you weren't aware of! We've seen many instances where only one person saw a potential problem, but because the team was open to listening to that person, it allowed the organization to deal with the issue before it became serious. We've also seen cases where that one person's sensing fell on deaf ears because others didn't want to hear the message—and this was to the eventual detriment of the organization. So as you ask people to share what they're seeing, be sure to acknowledge and listen to their contribution.

To take this tool one step further, you could post the results outside your office or in a commons room or in a shared file—so that all team members can weigh in on it. And as the team encounters new information, they can add it. In short, this tool could be a quick, inexpensive way to transparently communicate and share what the team is sensing, which may then drive conversations about what the factors mean and how to figure out responses.

TOOL 8.2: Coordinate and Define Your Sensing Activities

Now that you and your team have started to think about the factors that have influenced, are influencing, or could influence your work, let's talk about which factors warrant more or less attention. Ask your team two questions:

1. How likely it is that Factor X will occur?
2. How much will Factor X impact your work (if it occurs)?

Categorize each factor into one of the four cells in the matrix below. Remember that impact to your work could be both positive and negative. Technology is an example of a factor that can affect your work in a positive way, if you take advantage of it, or in a negative way, if the technology doesn't work.

If you previously listed each factor on a sticky note (or virtual sticky note), just rearrange the sticky notes into a two-by-two matrix. You might even use different color sticky notes to represent which category the factor lands in.

Coordinate and Define Your Sensing Activities

		Not Likely	Very Likely
Impact to Your Work	High Impact	**A** • Infrequent sensing • Respond with scenario-planning	**B** • Frequent sensing • Respond with pilots and experiments
	Low Impact	**C** • Infrequent sensing • Respond when needed	**D** • Frequent sensing • Respond with contingent operating procedures

Likelihood That the Factor Will Occur

Few resources should be devoted to preparing for unlikely events that have little impact on your work (those in cell C);

however, you should monitor those factors every now and then and recategorize them if they change. If your sensing reveals that a low-probability, low-impact event is starting to happen, you can begin to develop a response at that point.

Events that are unlikely but would have a large effect on your work (cell A factors) require sensing, and you should start preparing a response. Scenario-planning is a technique that is useful for this situation. You might walk your team through an exercise in which they examine an unlikely but impactful scenario so that they can generate a response. Scenario-planning not only helps to ensure that you're prepared, but also helps the team build responding skills. You probably don't need to carry out a full scenario-planning exercise each year for each factor in this cell, as long as the factor is unlikely to occur. Instead, consider rotating the factors your team chooses for scenario-planning. For example, if you identify six unlikely but impactful factors, run a scenario-planning exercise for two of them each year, so that you can examine every factor at least every third year. If your monitoring reveals clues that a factor might occur, then step up your monitoring and begin to pilot possible responses.

For factors that are likely but not impactful (cell D), monitor them to anticipate when they're most likely to occur. You might find ways to automate or routinize sensing these factors. For example, one team member could check on the factor each day (or each week or month, depending on the factor), or you could set up an automated alert to tell you when something has changed. Begin piloting responses based on what you know about the factor at the time, then repilot modified responses when the factor changes. Developing contingency procedures is an excellent way to address these factors while also helping less-experienced team members learn your standard processes. One example of a contingency procedure is a plan for how to handle a minor snowstorm: employees could work from home, a predesignated "snow day" team could go into the office to handle the day's work, or customers could be notified that a minor delay will occur.

Events that are likely and impactful (cell B) warrant both monitoring and response. Sensing the event can give you valuable insight into when the event will occur, so that you know how much time you have to prepare a response; then, regardless of how much time you have, your team should start piloting and experimenting to find possible responses immediately.

As you sense, you might learn that a factor has changed in such a way that it now belongs in a different cell. If this happens, adjust how it's being monitored to reallocate your team's time and attention more efficiently.

After you fill out the matrix, talk with your team about who will monitor each factor and prepare responses. That will help you make sure that a factor doesn't fall through the cracks or that, on the flip side, you don't have too many people spending time on a particular factor. To cement the routines, be sure that you don't treat them as a one-time exercise. Post the matrix so that the team can add and reorganize factors appropriately. Encourage and praise them when they keep it up to date. You could also incorporate the matrix into team meetings, asking team members to provide a quick update to new or changed factors.

TOOL 8.3: Sensing and Interpreting Checklists

Now that you have a better handle on which factors warrant closer attention and who will keep an eye on them, talk to your team members about ways to sense and interpret the factors. Use the checklists below to generate new ideas for sensing and interpreting activities. Check off activities that you think could help your team. Remember, some sensing may be reactive. But if you can become aware that a change is about to happen before it affects your work, you'll have more time to find a way to respond effectively.

Sensing and Interpreting Checklists

Checklist of Sensing Activities
☐ Check for updates to the organizational mission, strategic plans, objectives, and goals.
☐ Look for recent important decisions that have been made elsewhere in the organization.
☐ Ask leadership for advance notice on new organizational policies or rules.
☐ Ask customer-facing employees to share new challenges as they come up.
☐ Collect data and store it in a database, relying on automated tools or alerts (e.g., an alert when customer-satisfaction ratings drop below a defined level), if possible.
☐ Read books, journals, periodicals, and news stories.
☐ Listen to podcasts.
☐ Watch videos or documentaries.
☐ Monitor for new or proposed laws or regulations.
☐ Subscribe to industry newsletters or websites.
☐ Set up news feeds to alert you when articles about specific topics are published.
☐ Find compilations or summary reports from professional associations or industry groups.
☐ Create a "call a customer" or "reach out to an expert" initiative.
☐ Ask employees who attend a conference to give a presentation about what they learned.
☐ Other sensing activities that I can do: _____
☐ Other sensing activities that I can collaborate with others on: _____

Checklist of Interpreting Activities
☐ Talk with and listen to experts who are engaging in sensing.
☐ Foster conversations across levels (e.g., top-level leaders talking to mid-level leaders and individual contributors).
☐ Foster cross-organizational conversations by inviting people from other parts of the organization to your meetings and vice versa.
☐ Use artificial-intelligence tools (if available) or other methods to analyze data so that you can identify trends and patterns.
☐ Find new ways to visualize data to identify patterns and trends.
☐ Ask employees to present new information as a conversation starter at a team meeting.
☐ Consult with outside experts, such as academics, consultants, other agencies, vendors, industry expert panels, and industry and professional associations.
☐ Collect and curate information (e.g., papers, articles, books; lessons learned; notes from employees who've attended conferences or seminars) into a knowledge base.
☐ Convene customer panels to understand current and changing customer needs.
☐ Read trend reports published by industry or professional associations.
☐ Other interpreting activities that I can do: _____
☐ Other interpreting activities that I can collaborate on with others: ___

As you review the checklist, it will probably seem like a lot to do! That's why you need to rely on everyone in your organization to engage in some form of sensing. And you'll need to get them involved in interpreting what all of this information means for your work. Different people will naturally be drawn to sensing different topics, which is exactly what you want. Some people may focus on technology or their functional field, while others may stay up to date on current events or new laws or policies. Still others may prefer to learn about new techniques or approaches. Some people will naturally focus on what's going on within the organization, while others will focus on external happenings. Some of the topics that people focus on may seem directly related to the organization's mission, such as new organizational policies, while other topics may seem less directly related. What people focus on may change, too, as people's interests evolve. Make it clear that it's okay for them to sense in areas that are a bit farther afield of their immediate responsibilities, of course, as long as they are staying on top of their job.

When you first ask people to get involved in sensing, some will embrace it right away, while others may hold back to see whether you are serious. That's perfectly normal! Those who are reticent might be watching to see what happens to someone who spent fifteen minutes reading through customer feedback emails or perusing a new piece of legislation. By positively reinforcing those who are engaging in sensing, you are letting everyone know what is expected. When talking with employees, you might want to cover these points:

- It's okay to spend five to ten minutes a day gathering information, learning something new that falls outside your primary job duties, or having a discussion with someone to make sense of information, as long as doing these things doesn't interfere with getting your job done.
- It's up to you what information you spend time gathering or talking to others about.
- If you need to spend more than a few minutes a day on something, talk to your supervisor. He may be able to allow you to dig deeper on a specific topic. Planning and preparing for events that might occur and significantly affect the organization may require the investment of time

and other resources. In addition, coordinating with higher-level leaders is necessary to ensure access to resources to prepare for such events.

- Remember to use good judgment and follow organizational policies about what can and can't be shared with others, both within and outside the organization.
- To the extent possible, you are expected to share information—not hoard it.

Some employees may already be sensing, although they never thought of it as such. For example, sometimes an employee may take a few minutes to ask a customer about their upcoming needs. Other employees may belong to professional associations or subscribe to an industry newsletter and not realize that staying on top of industry trends and developments is a form of sensing!

Additional sensing ideas include creating outreach or integrator roles to stay on top of changes happening upstream and downstream from your team. Rotating these roles is yet another way to involve employees in sensing while also providing developmental opportunities. Perhaps start the ball rolling by assigning people (who you know are willing) to engage in specific sensing activities; then, when it's time to rotate in new sensing team members, ask for volunteers. Strategic-planning techniques can also help you sense what's happening and figure out what to pay attention to; these techniques include horizon-scanning and scenario-planning. For projects or one-time events, a premortem exercise can help you anticipate all the things that could go wrong so that you can adjust your project plan and actions accordingly. In a premortem exercise, a group is asked to imagine that everything went wrong with the project and then identify reasons why it did not succeed.

The wider the net you cast, the more you can stay on top of negative events as well as opportunities to improve

TOOL 8.3 (*continued*)

responsiveness. Casting a wide net does bring some risks—too wide a net can yield little actionable information, while too narrow a net can cause you to be blindsided by highly impactful events. So part of interpreting may be discussions on the risks and benefits of casting wide and finding the right balance. Devoting a little time to sensing topics that seem unrelated to your work might pay off at some point—a solution to a problem in a different field, for example, might help you solve current issues you are facing. The important thing is to encourage people to keep learning. Bringing different perspectives will help the organization come up with innovative ideas for improving effectiveness and efficiency and for solving new problems.

ENGAGE IN REACTIVE AND PROACTIVE SENSING

When you ask employees to play a role in sensing, you might point out that some sensing will be reactive—that is, they might sense a change after the fact—while other sensing will be proactive, intuiting change that is about to occur or might happen eventually. Both types of sensing are necessary, but most organizations will benefit by ramping up the amount of proactive sensing they are doing.

While some reactive sensing will occur, your goal is to minimize those instances and give your team as much lead time as possible to respond. While some events, such as snowstorms or power outages, catch organizations off guard, you can anticipate that these events will happen at some point. You might not know exactly when, but you can plan for a scenario in which people will be unable to work in your building. Even if a different event happened, such as a water outage, your plan would still apply, perhaps with just minor adjustments.

Similarly, you can prepare for internal events that you know will happen according to a regular schedule, such as the annual budget cycle, or at some undetermined point in the future, such as a data call or a new executive request to provide an introductory briefing about the organization's work. Assigning a team member the role of watching for these events is another way to help your employees learn and develop, especially as that role rotates.

BUILD IN TIME FOR INTERPRETATION

You also might need to allow for formal and informal interpreting. Again, both approaches will be needed to stay on top of a turbulent environment. Formal interpreting can be done by allocating time in weekly or monthly meetings to discuss changes that are happening or building in time as needed during project or strategic planning. Informal interpreting takes place when employees have impromptu conversations about what they are sensing, reinforced by knowledge sharing and learning norms and supported by a foundation of psychological safety.

As with sensing, employees should feel that it's acceptable to spend five to ten minutes a day on informal interpreting. They should be able to reach out to their colleagues in other parts or at other levels in the organization. Effective interpreting often requires leaders as well as individual contributors to come together to figure out what a change might mean for the mission. Interpreting takes time, and interpretations may eventually change as new information comes to light, as new people are brought into the sense-making conversation, and as everyone spends time thinking through what the information means. So if an employee doesn't immediately know what a piece of new information means, that's okay! It might take time to make sense of it.

ENGAGE IN REACTIVE AND PROACTIVE RESPONDING

Just as sensing can be reactive and proactive, so, too, can responding. After identifying factors that have shifted or may shift, and after making sense of what that shift means for the organization's mission and work, you'll want to develop a response.

When we think about responding, we usually think about reacting to changes that have already happened and now need to be dealt with. Usually, you find out that you need to respond reactively when it's too late or, at best, when you have very short notice. Obviously, this is not ideal, but some changes are difficult, if not impossible, to foresee. For well-defined processes, less impactful changes that have already happened can often be handled by senior experts; they can either address the unique cases or develop contingency-based job aids that give other employees clear guidance on how to handle new cases or requests. You may need to address more impactful changes with rapid experimentation aimed at quickly redefining a process; then once the new process is defined, employees supporting the process can be quickly trained.

Flexible processes are often designed to address minor contextual variations. Changes that have an unintended effect on a flexible process may also require a senior expert to mount a temporary or short-term response, while rapid experimentation finds a more permanent solution.

Even when a shift has been identified with sufficient advance notice, organizations do not always take steps to develop a response. This happens for many reasons—people are busy, for instance, or the resources needed to develop a response to something that may or may not happen are hard to secure, or leaders are focused on dealing with immediate situations and crises. Agile organizations, however, are highly proactive at figuring out responses in advance. Doing so gives the organization more time to test possible solutions and consult with experts. It also requires the organization to spend less on mounting a solution while incurring less risk. Even if the anticipated situation ends up not happening, proactively developing a response promotes learning and employee development and builds the capability for addressing future disruptions. Agile organizations often find that the solutions or capabilities that fall by the wayside become valuable when other changes happen in the future.

On-call teams are another way prepare to respond: designating specific team members to respond if an event happens. The team members would review and update the contingency plan and perhaps conduct a trial run, then agree to be available if the event occurs. The team members continue to work in their regular job while being on-call. Serving on such a team also helps your team as a whole to develop additional skills, especially when membership in the on-call team rotates, so that more people are prepared to respond.

MYTH: PROACTIVE ACTIONS MIGHT NOT PAY OFF

We sometimes hear the concern that being proactive simply takes people away from their job, wasting their valuable time with little payoff. The truth is that being purely reactive ensures ineffective responses and stressed employees. When changes happen without warning, people have to scramble to figure out what to do. Employees supporting well-defined processes may continue to apply the process even when it no longer applies, resulting in low-quality products or services, dissatisfied customers, and disgruntled employees.

We are not suggesting that organizations devote a majority of their resources to prepare for unlikely events. What we are suggesting is that organizations devote some portion of their resources to preparing for future events, allocating more resources to likely events and at least a small portion of resources to unlikely events. Doing so will get the organization out of constant reactive "firefighting" mode. Although it can be difficult to emerge from a state of constant crisis, there are some ways to do so:

- Identify employees who have bandwidth and get them involved in proactive sensing and responding. People might have time available for sensing and responding when a project is coming to an end or when a new project is starting. Also consider teaming with another unit or group to sense, interpret, and respond to similar factors. If your team doesn't have any bandwidth, perhaps the other team does.
- Identify portions of unused budgets and reallocate them to support rapid experiments. Although there might be constraints on when and how some money can be used, other funds with fewer constraints could be available.
- Rely on small teams to find inexpensive ways to test responses; prototypes can often be developed using common office supplies, and process improvements can often be tested using past

cases, with tabletop exercises, or by walking one or two current cases through a new process.

- Reinforce the norm that all employees should devote time to sensing and responding. We understand that many people are already overburdened, and we certainly don't want them to become even more stressed. However, employees should try to find their own routine for sensing and responding, whether that's five to ten minutes per day or thirty minutes on a Friday afternoon.

- Be sure to listen to employees, including the squeaky wheels. If you reframe their input as sensing, they might be telling you that something has changed that the organization has not yet responded to. You might ask employees to become part of the solution by collecting more information to understand the problem and piloting possible solutions.

- Review current processes to eliminate steps that add little or no value. In any organization, when something doesn't go as planned, checks and balances are added to prevent it from happening again. The drawback is that, over time, processes can become filled with unnecessary steps, resulting in their taking more time and effort to carry out. In many situations, this can drain more resources than the unlikely scenario they've been put in place to prevent! Ask employees where steps can be removed with minimal impact. Of course, pilot and refine the new approach before putting it into practice. In the end, people will have more time to devote to sensing and responding.

- Work with higher levels of management to secure funding for sensing and responding on specific topics. Many organizations devote funds for strategic planning; work with management to use some of those funds for proactive sensing to gather data on factors that are expected to affect the organization. Other funds, if available, could be used to support employees on temporary teams that form to address specific topics or factors.

- Expand your network of employees. If your immediate team is overburdened, consider how you can use interns, people on rotational assignments, temporary employees, or returning retirees to help you understand all of the changes affecting your unit.

The sooner you can spot likely future events as well as those that are unlikely but significant, the more time you will have to prepare a response. Your vigilance will enable you to keep your contingency response up to date. If the event has become less likely, put it on the back burner; if the event pops up again, you'll already have a starting point.

MYTH: EXPERIMENTING AND PILOTING MIGHT NOT PAY OFF

Some leaders tell us that they hesitate to try new approaches for fear that resources will be wasted if things don't go perfectly. We've seen many examples of organizations conducting a full-scale pilot for a new program or process, only to revert back to the old approach when the pilot doesn't go perfectly. The truth is that experiments and pilots should not go perfectly. If you already knew how to do something well, you'd already be doing it and the pilot would be pointless! The whole reason for conducting experiments and pilots is to learn how to improve a program or process, help employees build new skills, and build support for the improved approach.

An experiment or pilot should not be a full-scale program or process. Instead, start small and then build up as you refine them. Some organizations refer to the initial running of a new program as a pilot. If it goes well, then it's continued with little change (if it's not broken, don't fix it). If it doesn't go well, then the effort is scratched rather than refined, and the organization has taken on little risk. Try to avoid setting up your pilots as full-scale attempts at an initiative or program; instead, design them as a chance to test out essential features of the program. Make changes until the program has improved sufficiently. Only at that point should you pilot other aspects of the program, and even then, work as quickly and inexpensively as possible.

Blair continues to think about how to expand the routines into her team's work even more. As she's delegated more and more decisions to her team, they've become comfortable making those decisions, which is another sign that they have psychological safety. She doesn't always agree with their decisions, but she always backs them up. And she's been pleasantly surprised that their choices usually work out. A couple of times when things didn't work out, Blair felt that backing them up served to retain their trust and ensured that they learned from the experience.

The weekly team meeting has become an effective forum for decision-making, especially when the team knows which decisions need to be made and has the relevant information before the meeting. So Blair decided to run an expanded sensing exercise. With her team's and Ms. Barton's approval, Blair also invited Mrs. Banks to attend the next team meeting so that she could see firsthand how differently the team is operating. Blair's delighted that Mrs. Banks accepted the meeting invitation and joins the virtual room just as the meeting begins.

After welcoming Mrs. Banks, Blair starts the sensing exercise: "Back when we listed all of the things that affect our work, we were amazed by how many things we came up with. I don't think any of us knew how much is changing. Now I'd like to circle back with sensing and even dig a bit deeper."

This time, however, she doesn't ask them to individually list the events and circumstances that affect their work—because she's sure they're ready to tackle the discussion together. She pulls out a large pile of sticky notes and asks them to start writing down all of the things that have affected them in the past, are affecting them now, or that might affect them in the future. As they start writing, she draws three columns on the whiteboard and asks them to place the sticky notes in one of the columns.

As Vincent places his items on the whiteboard, he exclaims, "I see that someone wrote down that Congress could choose to change our entire agency's mission, which of course would affect all of our customers' contracting needs. I hadn't thought of that before!"

Blair advises the group to add a checkmark to others' sticky notes if they agree with it. Once they're finished, Blair says, "We need to make sure we monitor these, but we also need to get work done. Which factors do we think are more likely? And which factors would have the most impact to our work if it did occur?"

Mrs. Banks even weighs in: "You know, I get frequent updates about what's going on in various congressional subcommittees. I'd be glad to pass along any updates that I think are relevant. I didn't realize how forward thinking you're being and didn't know that you need advance notice in order to figure out how to adapt your work without bringing work to a halt. That seems like a better approach than what I had to do back when I was in your role."

After some discussion, the team starts to organize the factors into groups of likelihood and impact, which naturally leads to a conversation about where to focus their sensing and which factors merit preparing a response.

Barry says, "This is starting to make more sense now. We should spend a little bit of time on the things that won't affect us much or are unlikely. And we should spend a lot of time on things that will really affect us or are pretty likely. It's hard to predict the future, which means that we should revisit these things from time to time. We might need to up our focus on something that looks like it will really happen after all or spend less time on something that is going away."

"That's exactly right, Barry!" Blair says. "Let's look at these checklists of sensing and interpreting activities to get us thinking about the things we could be doing to stay on top all of this change."

The team begins to assign specific topics to different team members so that they can coordinate their sensing. They talk about how they could take turns giving five-minute "sensing updates" each week. They then ask Blair if they can spend another few minutes talking about what the observed signals mean for their work, which would help them plan experiments.

A couple weeks later, just when Blair feels that her team has a good grip on all of the factors, a bunch of unanticipated events happen all in the same week. A couple of her team's largest customers have a sudden change in direction, requiring some quick-turnaround contracting just when they're getting ready for several new solicitations. At the same time, a new, highly visible program kicks off, requiring significant contracting support. The team is struggling to keep up when all of a sudden several highly experienced team members need to take personal leave.

Blair is adamant about not simply expecting people to work extra hours, so she reaches out to other contracting teams for help. One team provides an experienced team member who just transferred from another agency and didn't have a permanent assignment yet. Another team sends two high-potential team members who are looking for opportunities to learn about other types of contracts. Several of Blair's team members step up into temporary roles that they had cross-trained for. It is clear that the new process, although a few kinks are still being worked out, is making them much more efficient. Blair thinks, "This was a long two months, but it could have been so much more stressful. My sensing about being able to use other teams was beneficial because of the relationships that I established with them; I know that my team will pay them back while also benefitting from the expanded experience. We actually came out ahead from this unanticipated stress test by allowing people to gain experience in new roles, and they did wonderfully because the whole team shared their expertise and supported them. The rhythm that we started many months ago also paid off; we were ready for this challenge with our streamlined meeting format and delegated decision-making. And all of this was possible because I worked at building up their psychological safety."

NINE

Invest in People

A couple of months later, Blair is starting to think about how much her team has built new skills and learned new ways to carry out their work. But they still have a long way to go. Just the other day, when they were updating the list of factors that could impact their work, the team started to talk about gaps in their knowledge and skills. Their discussion was focused on how to bring every team member up to the same level on their core skills while having a few team members concentrate on mastering specific skills that could be valuable in the future.

Although each person on the team, including Blair, must complete a certain number of training hours each year, the budget to attend formal training always seemed limited.

"Also, some people on the team would get a lot out of going to a class," Blair thinks, "While other people just need to get more experience—and get it quickly. And for other gaps that we have, I don't even think formal classes are the way to go. I wonder what other ways there are to build up our skills quickly while not spending a lot of money."[1]

People are an essential resource in an agile organization. They use their expertise and experience to carry out agility routines, make

---

1. Jamie Ann Neidig contributed to this chapter.

decisions, share information, and take action. Agile organizations invest in their employees because they know that underwriting will help the organization prepare for changes and solve both old and new problems that arise.

As the environment changes in new, complex ways, it's hard to know ahead of time all of the tasks that employees will need to carry out. You may not even know the full list of skills that they will need, especially with rapidly evolving technologies. But you can anticipate that employees will constantly need to both learn new things and have the time to reflect and renew in order to carry out the organization's mission effectively and efficiently.

INVEST IN CONTINUAL EMPLOYEE DEVELOPMENT

In an agile organization, employee development is viewed as an essential investment rather than a cost. While it can be tempting to put employee development on the back burner or decide that employees should invest in themselves on their own time, agile organizations place a priority on employee development. That development pays off in several ways—employees are engaged, excited by, and motivated to carry out their work; they remain with the organization longer; they display higher individual and team performance; and they create the foundation for innovation. When the organization helps employees develop, employees feel valued— because they are valued. Retaining employees yields several benefits, including less time and resources on hiring and onboarding; it also results in a knowledgeable, experienced workforce who already understands your norms and environment. When employees engage in learning, they also carry out many of the activities that we've discussed, such as sensing, interpreting, and developing their knowledge network.

Agile organizations devote monetary resources to training employees. Sometimes, the best way for you or a team member to learn is to take a training course, a certification course, or even a college class. We encourage that type of learning as long as you and they screen out insubstantial courses and classes. If you need assistance finding the right course or class, ask an expert for help, such as a senior person in your organization or a professor at a local university. If formal training is a good option, then consider whether you or your team member plan to apply it to the job. It's okay to do the training even if you think you won't need to apply the material immediately—as long as you are confident that you will use it in the near future. And remember that agile organizations invest quite a bit in people skills as well as technical and functional skills. For example, a budget analyst might benefit from learning about negotiation tactics, or an IT analyst might provide better customer service after acquiring skills from a communication class. When a course or class is the right solution, be sure to get the most out of it by sharing some of what you learned with the rest of the team—ideally in a hands-on way, not just in a slide-based debrief. And make sure to document the courses and results in a prominent place so that others can benefit from it later. Not only will the documentation help you justify your budgets, but it will also help you with longitudinal tracking of skills development.

This approach doesn't mean that you need a large training budget. Although there may be some instances where it makes sense for you or one of your team members to attend a training class or to pursue a certification, much employee development can be done inexpensively with a bit of forethought, such as through cross-training or rotating roles. Considerable learning occurs on the job, and classroom-based learning works best when the material is reinforced on the job. Low-cost ways to develop employees, in addition to traditional methods such as training and mentoring, include the following:

- Cross-training employees in related skills
- Pairing more experienced employees with less experienced employees to carry out certain tasks (known as work shadowing)
- Providing guided experience by way of an employee with expertise in a certain topic helping another employee learn the topic

- Rotating jobs across roles within a team or across teams
- Defining temporary or acting roles
- Having a team member lead a temporary or permanent team (as long as the employee doesn't feel they're being taken advantage of by taking a higher-level role without being fairly compensated)
- Creating communities of practice where employees from across the organization with expertise in and passion for a subject matter or technical area pass on knowledge, share best practices, and answer questions via in-person get-togethers, emails, or online groups
- Encouraging self-study using free or low-cost resources, such as articles, association newsletters and publications, academic journals, or online books that are purchased individually or through the organization's subscription
- Encouraging volunteer work at professional associations or chapters or at community organizations
- Promoting the idea of serving as a reviewer for journals, newsletters, or conferences
- Suggesting opportunities to give presentations to local professional groups, volunteer groups, and internal teams
- Creating paired work experiences, which allow two or more employees to gain knowledge of a function or activity together through trial and error, to leverage shared explicit knowledge to learn, and then to apply tacit knowledge.

You should expect all employees to engage in some form of development. Whether they support stable or flexible processes, employees need to develop, albeit in different ways. Those supporting stable processes may focus on continuing to develop process-improvement skills (e.g., six sigma or process mapping), while those supporting flexible processes might focus on learning innovation techniques (e.g., design thinking). Both types of employees can benefit from advancing their technical or functional skills as well as their people skills. In fact, agile organizations place a strong emphasis on employees developing their teamwork and communication skills, which are essential for sensing and interpreting and sharing knowledge. Leadership skills can be developed at all levels, as appropriate for the role. And agile organizations find that the skill everyone needs is the willingness and ability to learn.

Employee development also sets the foundation for innovation. More specifically, research shows that organizations that place an emphasis on training and that formally document people's developmental progress tend to be more innovative. In other words, creating an atmosphere where learning is expected and supported and where people become more competent pays off when your team comes up with novel ideas and solutions to both old and new problems. How does this happen? When people gain new skills, they are likely to uncover solutions to new problems or find new solutions to existing problems. Sometimes people draw connections between a new idea or technique that they recently learned about and a problem that they are experiencing on the job and come up with new insights. Seemingly unrelated information can bring new ways of thinking about problems, which then lead to new experiments. Learning experiences can also help employees enhance their professional networks, which can lead to new insights as well.

Effective employee development is linked to reduced turnover, which is often what organizations desire, because turnover is disruptive and expensive. Although you want to control turnover as much as possible, a couple of situations exist where it can play a valuable role. One situation is when someone on your team wants to transfer to another part of the organization to further grow their skills or advance their career. Even though you may miss having their skills and working with them personally, the whole organization benefits by providing growth opportunities. Consider how the employee adds to your knowledge network. Find ways to include the employee when sensing, interpreting, and responding overlaps between your team and the employee's new team. And extend an offer for the employee to return to your team, in either the same or a different role.

Another situation is when an employee wishes to leave your organization because their career goals are no longer aligned with the mission. You can try to find them a different role that meets their career goals, but if that is not possible, make sure to extend an offer to return should their goals re-align. In the rare instance that the employee is not agreeing with the agility principles, it may be best to part ways.

PROMOTE A LEARNING ORIENTATION

Cultivating a learning orientation will not only help your organization become more agile, but it may also support individuals in their career trajectories. Research indicates that having a learning orientation correlates both with promotion potential and leadership potential. Research also shows that creating an environment that supports learning and development is more likely to yield innovative ideas.

An essential skill for employees in agile organizations is the ability to learn quickly. And those with the view of "I don't want to learn anything else" do not fare well in an agile organization. So when selecting employees, take into account their views on and their track record of learning. You want people on your team who are curious, excited, and able to adapt their approach as their circumstances change, since your organization's environment is also changing all the time.

For existing employees, expect them to learn on the job. If someone has time available while waiting for a new project to start or a spare half hour on a Friday afternoon, expect them to use that time learning something relevant to their work. You could suggest they take advantage of resources, such as blogs or podcasts, that are aimed at learning in bite-size chunks. Or ask them to create their own repository where they can store resources and information to read later (and to share with others). Make them aware that sometimes insights occur when you're reading something different or taking time to refresh and reenergize. And be sure to set a good example by sharing with your team all of the new things that you are learning. Of course, not everyone will be on board, so when faced with a skeptical employee, try to gently convince them to learn (and share) at least one small piece of new information.

Having a learning plan for your team can also be helpful. A learning plan can be very simple—you can find one topic or skill—even if it is small—that your team can begin to learn about. Or consider something that you have little knowledge of and that would help your work. It could also be something more formal and complex—for example, individual development plans, budgetary requests for training—depending on what works best for your team and internal processes.

While you don't need a detailed, labor-intensive plan, it will help to know who is learning what and how that aligns with what your team needs to know now and in the future. Your team will also benefit by knowing what skills you and other team members are trying to develop. Consider asking your team to share their learning plans; you can get them started by sharing your own. For transparency, post the learning plans where they are accessible throughout the year. Try to focus and prioritize learning, but don't neglect the long shots; spending time to better understand those low-probability, but potentially impactful events, that may occur in the future can pay off in surprising ways.

You may also wish to set aside a regular meeting time for the team to share quick updates on their current learning journeys. Through this sharing, you will likely discover that different employees embrace different ways of learning: one employee may prefer to read books or articles (sensing), while another may enjoy participating in interpreting conversations, and yet another may relish carrying out experiments. All of these learning methods are valuable. But after just a short time, you will probably be amazed at how much learning has taken place. Remember to take time to acknowledge and celebrate all of the effort that others have put into learning.

One term for sharing what you are learning with your team is *public learning*. Talking about what you are learning, where you are struggling, and how your new insights might change your current approach will help employees better understand that it is okay for them to do this too. You are also demonstrating that no one needs to be an expert in everything; there is always room for more knowledge.

At the organizational level, one way to ramp up when specific skills are needed quickly is creating talent pools. A talent pool is a database of internal or external candidates that have specific skills the organization may need at a given time. Talent pools are usually more of an inventory of individuals' skills than an assessment, and they are not tied to performance management. They give the organization flexibility when a skill is needed for a relatively short time. A pool of people with a new skill can be created through cross-training as well as hiring contingent employees (e.g., contractors, temporary workers, on-call retirees), which gives the organization faster access to the specific skill sets it needs than if it were to create new positions and then hire people to fill them. It is also a way to ramp down quickly when the skill is no longer needed; current employees can go back to their regular jobs having learned or developed a skill, and contingent employees can return to the talent pool.

We recognize that government agencies must adhere to human resource laws and policies. However, those laws and policies are changing and, no doubt, will continue to change. So we encourage leaders to communicate and collaborate with their HR and agency leaders to influence changes to laws and policies in a way that will give agencies the flexibility they need while also supporting merit principles. Moreover, we encourage HR leaders to demonstrate agility by seeking out innovative solutions to meet strategic HR objectives (of course, complying with relevant laws). We also encourage public sector leaders to approach HR professionals with a problem to be solved rather than with a requested solution. That way, both parties can work together to solve the problem, even if the solution the leader had in mind was not viable within HR policies.

TOOL 9.1: Document (and Celebrate) Learning

Ask your team to fill in the table below (or use sticky notes) to help identify (1) what learning looks like in your organization and (2) what to focus on in the coming months.

Document (and Celebrate) Learning

A year ago, what did we not know? What were we unable to do?	What did we learn? How did we learn it?
Right now, what do we not know? What are we unable to do?	What can we learn? How can we learn it?

Be sure to acknowledge and express pride for all of the information and wisdom that you and your team have gained. Use this as an opportunity to reinforce agility norms by giving them specific, positive feedback about what they've learned and how that has been valuable.

PROACTIVELY IDENTIFY FUTURE SKILLS

Agile organizations are highly proactive at identifying future skills that their workforce will need. That's because, with things changing rapidly, human capital strategies that were once updated every few years now need to be updated more frequently—sometimes even on an ongoing basis. To identify the skills that the organization needs to have, you can rely on sensing and experimenting.

For example, if someone on your team discovers a new piece of software that could be adapted to your work, that's a signal you might need expertise in using the software in the near future. You can respond to this signal by asking a team member to learn more about the software and how to use it—perhaps by watching a free webinar offered by the software vendor, reading more about it, or talking to a colleague at another organization who has used it. As the team member builds knowledge about the software, she can help you decide whether it might be useful to your work. If you decide to purchase the software, you might be able to negotiate for training from the vendor. If vendor training isn't available, you could send employees to training courses to learn the software. Other ways to support employee learning would be to give them time to experiment with the software or to create an internal user group where experts throughout your organization provide help.

There are several ways to use sensing and experimenting to identify skills that your team might need. Here are a few of them:

- Read industry or association newsletters about trends.
- Review other organizations' job listings or recruiter websites.
- Conduct experiments that reveal new skills.
- Talk to colleagues throughout the organization about how they address similar challenges or problems.
- Review federal government data about occupations that are on the rise.
- Ask your team for their ideas on skills likely to become important in the future.

As with any type of sensing, you might find that your prediction doesn't pan out. So you'll want to find a balance between monitoring to see if the new skill will really be needed and rapidly investing in developing it. Obviously, you don't want to overinvest or invest too early, because doing so could use up resources that you need to invest in skills your team actually needs. So keep an eye on the skills you think you might need and, if you get to a point where you realize you'll need them, ramp up investment as slowly as the situation allows. Agile organizations find that even small investments in learning sometimes have big payoffs when unexpected events occur. For example, perhaps you asked an employee to research a new trend that is affecting your customers, and the employee gathered several industry reports and presented a summary at a learning hour. Then a few months later, a different unit mentions they're seeing the trend affect their customers—only now it's a huge problem and they need a solution fast. That small investment your team member made could help both teams figure out a solution much faster than if everyone were starting from scratch.

Finally, if you discover the need for a new skill at a time when you are also hiring, consider adding it as a required or preferred skill in the job description being advertised. Then, before you hire, make sure that you have the right position for the employee with the new skill. Remember that as skills change rapidly, human resource departments can have a hard time keeping up, especially with the constraints they face, so you may need to be proactive in how you work with them—for instance, by creating job descriptions and job titles that reflect new skills in the labor market.

PROVIDE TIME FOR EMPLOYEES TO RECHARGE AND REFRESH

Investing in your people means not only promoting their learning and development but also making sure that they feel valued. You can do many things to show employees that they are valued. You can make sure they are free to be themselves at work and to be curious and ask questions. You can also foster a space where employees feel comfortable learning from each other and sharing their diverse experiences, which creates conditions where ideas can emerge, solutions can form, and opportunities for sensing and interpreting can happen.

You can also invest in people by making sure they take the time they need to maintain their health and mental well-being, to care for family members, and to refresh their energy. Unfortunately, in some organizations, it's a badge of honor for people to work excessive hours over the long run or to never take a vacation. However, that leads to burnt out, stressed employees who do not bring their best to the job. It can also indicate that employee development is not a priority, sending the message that those who put in the most hours are the ones who gain the most experience, while others are not afforded the chance to develop and therefore contribute in more meaningful ways. We're not suggesting that people be allowed to slack off, but we are saying that people need time away from work to recharge.

Make sure that they take time off in a way that works for them, whether that's a vacation or a series of long weekends. Check in with them if they are working on a busy or stressful project and anticipate when they might need help. When someone finishes a complex, fast-paced project, find a way for him to spend a few days wrapping up the effort, which can provide him with closure and a chance to reflect on his accomplishments before he jumps into a new project. And continue to develop your team so that you don't force someone into an unnecessarily stressful situation where she is the only one who knows how to carry out a certain task.

Investing in people in this manner is likely to yield returns in daily productivity, and when a truly unforeseen event happens, your team will be better positioned to respond in terms of their knowledge, skills, and energy. When your team comes up with creative solutions on the fly, you might think they've pulled off a miracle, but they're actually just the engaged and highly developed team that you prepared to tackle anything.

MYTH: WE DON'T HAVE THE TIME OR MONEY TO DEVELOP EMPLOYEES

Agile organizations place a high priority on employee development, and they back it up with training and development dollars so that employees can take college classes, attend professional training courses, participate in leadership development programs, and benefit from coaching and mentoring. Understandably, however, very few organizations have the luxury of hosting slack resources; they don't have spare budget dollars or extra employees sitting on a bench just in case they are needed. That said, it's a myth that developing employees requires a large budget. Organizations with any type of budget can still find ways to inexpensively support employee development; indeed, we've already shared many of those ways in this chapter.

A related myth is that it's impossible to get ahead of the curve timewise—that once employees are in reactive mode, it's impossible for them to find time to participate in agility routines. We agree that it's hard to transition from a purely reactive mode to being more proactive. When employees are in purely reactive mode, they are subject to burnout and stress. In turn, burnt out, stressed employees are more likely to make errors and may choose to leave the organization, taking their knowledge with them, which, of course, further perpetuates reactive mode.

To help employees get out in front of all of the changes that are burning them out, you'll need to find ways for them to carry out routines in a manner that doesn't require them to simply work more hours. When they carry out the routines, they are also developing because they are learning new things through sensing and interpreting as well as through working more efficiently and effectively through responding. That said, here are ideas for finding time for your team to engage in routines while also supporting their professional development:

- Be intentional when assigning work; give assignments that provide new experiences and help build or expand existing skills.

- When planning projects, allow time for agility routines; expect project teams to apply these routines as part of their day-to-day work.
- Eliminate activities that add little value. These often include unnecessary reviews, approvals, and oversight; unproductive meetings with too many attendees; and burdensome documentation and plans.
- Make sure to spend time only on activities that add value, even if that value is not immediately apparent, including the agility routines and employee development.

As Blair continues her train of thought about how to invest in her team, she runs into Hank, who asks her for her thoughts on training courses.

Hank says, "I learned a lot by researching the vendor tools. It's something I'd like to learn even more about. I hadn't realized how important cybersecurity is for the work we do and whatever tools we end up using. I know that we need to get a certain number of training hours each year. What if I continue to build my IT and cybersecurity skills?"

Blair smiles approvingly. "That's a great idea! I think these tools are going to be increasingly valuable to us in the future. Having someone who understands them from a technology and security perspective will help us be proactive. We don't want to buy something that has poor security. And we certainly don't want to be on the receiving end of a cyber-attack and have no one with the skills to deal with it."

Later in the day, Blair stops by Barb's team meeting just to listen in and see where they might need support as they continue to experiment with the new process. The discussion quickly turns to questions that they still have about the two leading tools. After hearing several great points, the team discusses possible experiments to answer the remaining questions.

Blair adds, "In a short period of time, you've learned an incredible amount. You've found really creative ways to learn the pros and cons of each tool with some really brief tests. And that knowledge is starting to guide the new process. And we got some positive recognition from Mrs. Banks for Hank's and Kyle's help to the western division last month when they started their search for a new requirements-management system. Hank, you and Kyle were able to suggest a tool that you ran across, pass along a contact to the vendor, and even give them some questions to ask. That saved the western division an incredible amount of time."

Barb jumps in. "And we've learned so much from our experiments. When one or two of us learn something and share it, we all benefit. Kyle, remember when you started using the new tool, and every time you uploaded the appendices, it crashed? I'm glad we figured out early on that we need to ask the programs for the information in a certain format. And then Hank figured out an easy fix to their file-storage system, which he wouldn't have known to do unless he had just read about it in that acquisition software blog. It would have been pretty disastrous for our customers if we had rolled out the new tool without knowing the file format."

Blair expands on Barb's point. "I'm devoting resources to making sure we all get the training and development we need for our current work and especially for investing widely in what we expect to do in the future. Sometimes that might mean taking a class or getting a certification. We probably don't have enough money for every class, but we can be smart about where we spend our training budget. And there are many other ways to make sure we expand our skills and continue to learn through the work that we're doing. We should keep sharing what we learn, changing up our roles so that people learn all aspects of the standard approach or become specialized in the new, more responsive approach. You know, we can also expand beyond our team by participating in the agency's job-rotation program or proposing our own rotation program with some of the other divisions. We can keep sensing like we've been doing. We will continue to have conversations about changes that we are sure will affect us so that we can invest in developing skills that we need in the future."

TEN

Putting It All Together

Blair walks down the familiar hallway to her office. It's been two years since she started her team on their agility journey. In a couple of weeks, Blair will be taking on a new role in the acquisition department. She's been asked to expand the agility journey to other acquisition teams. It's a great opportunity, and even Mrs. Banks is on board now, yet Blair recognizes that her current team is still working on building its own agility. While the team has made a lot of progress, she has come to realize that cultivating an entire agency for agility is an ongoing process, not a destination that can be arrived at. The team has learned how to reflect on and celebrate their successes while continuing on their journey forward.

By now, we hope that you, too, have made good progress, even if you and your team still have a way to go. We hope that you recognize that agility is an ongoing trek that is never fully complete. Implementing all of the ideas that we've shared is not something that will happen overnight. It may take many months—maybe years— to make new routines and actions stick.

If you've started on the journey, be sure to document your team's progress and to track relevant metrics so you're seeing the results you want. These metrics might include individual and team productivity, error rates, customer service scores, engagement scores, and turnover rates.

And if you haven't started your journey, remember that we don't expect you to be able to do everything we've outlined, to do it all at once, or to take it on alone. However, you will need to begin somewhere. This book is meant to be a hands-on guide, so use it as such. Circle back to chapters 1 and 2 and begin paying attention to your team's psychological safety. Then take action, whether it's starting a discussion about psychological safety or setting aside a few minutes to encourage a team member who has shared information appropriately.

But regardless of whether you're beginning or continuing your journey, we want to give you a few final pieces of parting advice.

BE PERSISTENT AND CONSISTENT

Yes, doing all of this is a big job. It may not go well at first. There will be ups and downs. Despite what happens, the worst thing you can do is to give up and go back to old ways. Reverting to old ways when things get challenging only tells people that you weren't serious.

The next worst thing you can do is to tackle only the easy or surface-level things—if you do only some of the "agility" things, you risk confusing people, creating burnout over the idea of agility, and misaligning the organization. In any organization, all parts are interrelated—structure, processes, roles, norms, people and their skills, and leadership. Therefore a change to one part of the organization requires changes to other parts so the system can continue to work in alignment.

If things aren't working as well as you'd like, then revisit the beginning of the process by looking at psychological safety. Ask yourself whether psychological safety is an issue. You might feel that things are safe, but others may not. Seek out your team's opinion. Pay close attention to their actions, looking for clues about how they are perceiving the situation.

If you truly believe that sufficient psychological safety exists, then take it one step further by facilitating open conversations with your team about it. Consider starting the process by talking to a few trusted team members individually to get a sense of the rest of the team's views on the psychological well-being and perceptions of the team. Next, try initiating dialogue with your entire team. Start talking openly about trust issues that have likely never been a topic of conversation before. Although you can't go back and change the experiences that have detracted from people's ability to feel safe and try new things, you can empathize with them and commit to running your team differently in the future, as long as you're getting the necessary results. You'll know you've made progress when they recognize that your intent isn't simply to add to their workload but to help them approach that workload in a way that produces better outcomes.

Remember that not everyone will jump on board at once. It may take time for everyone to get to the point where they feel safe enough to start engaging in agility routines. But you can start moving forward with those who are ready, which will help bring along those who are reticent by showing that it really is okay to approach work differently.

CYCLE BACK THROUGH THE CHAPTERS

Because different team members may be moving ahead with agility at different rates, cycle back through the chapters as you work to align your organization with all of the changes going on around it. We know it will be overwhelming to try to do everything! It is unlikely that everything will go perfectly, which is okay and expected. You do need to give it a genuine effort though. This doesn't mean that you have to solve every problem yourself or have all of the answers. Your role is to lead, guide, and coach your team to approach work in a new way together, which also means talking through what works and what doesn't.

By revisiting the chapters as you continue through the different phases of your agility journey, points that perhaps didn't resonate with you early on might make more sense later. Or you might find that certain topics become more relevant as your team becomes more agile. Although our suggestions are based on evidence, they are not a checklist of action items you can execute in a linear fashion. Rather, we suggest approaching actions iteratively and applying learnings from one set of new behaviors to the next set your team decides to address.

EXPAND YOUR APPLICATION

Although we've given you several suggestions, ideas, and recommendations, we know that it would be impossible for us to think of everything. Based on your own situations and organizational culture, you will surely find new ways to apply our advice. Each organization and situation are somewhat different; therefore, implement these ideas in a way that makes sense for you.

In particular, at some point on your journey, you may need to expand the principles beyond your team. For example, it might be hard for your team to become truly agile if your boss doesn't provide you with enough psychological safety. Similarly, if your team isn't leading with agility and providing psychological safety to their direct reports, little change will occur. And your unit's agility might be constrained by other units that are not yet agile themselves. In situations like these, you may need to expand your reach to other parts of the organization. Perhaps start by sharing with others that you've started on a journey toward agility. As you share about your team's progress, you can offer to help them get started as well; begin by talking about the importance of psychological safety. If a higher-level leader or even a peer expresses some of the myths we've covered, you can use the research-based truths provided to encourage them.

In addition, much of the advice and many of the tools that we've presented just scratch the surface of all there is to know about these topics. So we encourage you to find additional resources—books, articles, training courses, classes, podcasts, videos—that can help you continue to develop your "agility muscles." Some of the topics we've introduced that you might want to learn more about include effective decision-making, knowledge sharing, process improvement, divergent thinking techniques, effective meeting management, critical conversations, human resource planning, and employee development.

We wish you the best of luck on your journey toward agility!

Looking back on the journey, Blair thinks, "We've really come a long way. And we did it as a team. Our customers give us rave reviews now. We've increased the number of contracts we process while reducing errors. Our employee engagement scores have dramatically increased. The team members genuinely seem to enjoy their work and have received recognition for our innovative approaches. Hank and Kyle even received an award for best presentation at the annual acquisition conference. The team just feels a lot different now. We address issues head-on rather than letting them fester and then erupt. I love hearing people express different viewpoints and then work together to find solutions that work for everyone. I'm really glad to see their careers grow. A few of them moved on to larger roles and positions with more responsibility because of how much they developed as professionals. They've become allies in my knowledge network, which I rely on to sense what's happening in other parts of the agency.

"Of course, there have been plenty of bumps along the way. A few people on my team were pretty resistant but finally came around once they realized that agility meant figuring out how we can accomplish our mission together—that it was not just me telling them to do things a new way. Some people got on board right away, and others took a bit longer but came around after a combination of persistence, straightforward one-on-one conversations to address their concerns, and adjustments to find the right role for them. One or two people even decided early on that agility wasn't for them, but I found roles for them in another group. And we had to build up our 'muscle' for learning how to run experiments; we had many things not go well, but at least that happened during a test, so we headed off some potential big failures."

Blair now feels confident in Barb, who will be taking over for Blair and will help the team continue its journey. And as for her own agility journey, Blair knows that it will continue in her new role.

Appendix

ORGANIZATIONAL AGILITY FRAMEWORK

As we began developing the organizational agility framework, we tracked down and reviewed numerous research studies that examined some aspect of organizational agility. While reading through all of this research, we grouped the concepts (i.e., the variables or levers) examined in each study by similarity. Those three major groupings follow:

1. The organization's *environment,* which includes all of the changing factors that the organization must deal with, both internal and external.
2. Actions that the organization can take to better manage the swirl of change in its environment, which we further divided into *agility routines* (i.e., sensing, interpreting, and responding routines) and *levers* (i.e., ways the organization can approach its work differently to support the routines).
3. *Outcomes* that show the organization is effectively managing the changes that occur.

Together these three groupings make up our organizational agility framework, which is shown in Figure A.1. Supporting references that document the importance and relevance of each part of the framework are shown in figure A.2–A.5.

Figure A.1: *Organizational Agility Framework*

When we consult with organizations on how to enhance their organizational agility, this framework guides our thinking and advice. It would not be effective to try to change an organization by working on one lever at a time, however. Rather, when we work with an organization, our guidance follows the same order as the chapters in this book. Note that psychological safety does not appear in our framework as a separate dimension; instead, it runs throughout each of the routines and levers.

In figure A.2 below, we describe the variables for each of the three groupings and present the references we drew on to create the framework.

THE ENVIRONMENT

Our framework includes the external and internal environment. The external environment comprises factors outside the organization, such as changes to legislation, social factors and trends, customer or citizen expectations, technology, and natural events. The internal environment includes factors within an organization that affect a specific group or area inside that organization.

The External Environment	
The external environment consists of factors outside the organization that influence or affect the organization, including (a) legislative and political changes, (b) social factors and trends, (c) customer/citizen expectations, (d) technology, and (e) naturally occurring events.	Alavi et al., 2014; Boin & van Eeten, 2013; Butler & Surace, 2015; De Florio, 2014; Dyer & Shafer, 2003; Fleming, 2012; Hamel & Välikangas, 2003; Harraf et al., 2015; Holbeche, 2015; Jaaron & Backhouse, 2014; Pellissier, 2012; Sharifi & Zhang, 1999; Zhang, 2011
The Internal Environment	
The internal environment consists of factors within the organization that affect a specific group or area in the organization, including its leadership, its policies, its interactions with other groups, and its economic/financial situation.	Corporate Executive Board, 2014; Holsapple & Li, 2008

Figure A.2: *The Environment*

THE ORGANIZATION: AGILITY ROUTINES AND LEVERS

Our literature review found that agile organizations engage in routines and enact certain levers to support those routines. In agile organizations, everyone is involved in sensing and interpreting routines as well as responding routines (see Figure A.3). These routines are second nature to people in agile organizations.

Sensing & Interpreting Routines	
All employees are involved in systematically, proactively, and routinely collecting information about the environment and engaging in constructive debate, reflection, and analysis about the effect of changes or potential changes. Employees continually scan the environment, often using technology, to gather information from outside and inside the organization, including from stakeholders, customers, outside experts, and other organizations.	Alavi et al., 2014; Boin & van Eeten, 2013; Breu et al., 2002; Brueller et al., 2014; Butler & Surace, 2015; Cegarra-Navarro et al., 2016; Corporate Executive Board, 2014; De Florio, 2014; Doz & Kosonen, 2010; Dyer & Shafer, 2003; Edmondson, 1999, 2012; Felipe et al., 2016; Hamel & Välikangas, 2003; Harraf et al., 2015; Holsapple & Li, 2008; Hopkin, 2015; Moynihan, 2012; Nejatian & Zarei, 2013; Overby et al., 2006; Sambamurthy et al., 2003; Schwandt, 1995; Sharifi & Zhang, 1999; Sutcliffe et al., 1999; Teece et al., 2016; Weick & Sutcliffe, 2015; Worley et al., 2014
Responding Routines	
All employees are involved in making decisions and taking action to respond to changes in the environment. This includes responding in new ways, as needed. The organization may also take actions to anticipate changes in the environment.	Alavi et al., 2014; Boin & van Eeten, 2013; Breu et al., 2002; Brueller et al., 2014; Cegarra-Navarro et al., 2016; Corporate Executive Board, 2014; Felipe et al., 2016; Hamel & Välikangas, 2003; Harraf et al., 2015; Holbeche, 2015; Holsapple & Li, 2008; Hopkin, 2015; Lewis et al., 2015; Mahmoudi, 2015; Moynihan, 2012; Overby et al., 2006; Sharifi & Zhang, 1999

Figure A.3: *Agility Routines*

Our research review also found that the organization must carry out work in a manner that supports agility routines. We identified seven levers that leaders can use to change the way work is organized (see figure A.4):

1. Organizational structure
2. Knowledge sharing and experimentation
3. Decision-making practices
4. Leader actions
5. Processes
6. Roles
7. Norms and expectations

Each lever includes aspects of both stability and flexibility.

Organizational Structure	
Stability is provided by a formal structure that is unchanging and flat; employees are assigned to functional groups in order to guide their growth and development.	Aghina et al., 2015; Alavi et al., 2014; Argyris & Schon, 1996; Boin & van Eeten, 2013; Butler & Surace, 2015; De Florio, 2014; Dyer & Shafer, 2003; Edmondson, 2012; Galbraith, 2014; Harraf et al., 2015; Holbeche, 2015; Holsapple & Li, 2008; Jaaron & Backhouse, 2014; Lewis et al., 2015; O'Reilly & Tushman, 2004; Orton & Weick, 1990; Sutcliffe et al., 1999; Teece et al., 2016; Worley et al., 2014
Flexibility is provided by supplementing the formal structure with both leader-directed teams as well as self-organizing and self-managing teams that form, reform, and dissolve in order to sense, understand, and respond to the environment. Power and authority are decentralized.	

Knowledge Sharing and Experimentation	
Employees openly share information, communicate, and collaborate, enabling them to learn quickly. They conduct rapid experiments and tests on possible new services or improvements to current services. Employees integrate results from experiments into processes. Employees engage in formal and informal routines to search for, share, and retain information from the environment and from the results of experiments.	Aghina et al., 2015; Alavi et al., 2014; Argyris & Schon, 1996; Barbaroux, 2011; Boin & van Eeten, 2013; Breu et al., 2002; Butler & Surace, 2015; Cegarra-Navarro et al., 2016; Corporate Executive Board, 2014; Davenport & Prusak, 2000; de Oliveira et al., 2012; Doz & Kosonen, 2010; Dyer & Shafer, 2003; Edmondson, 1999, 2012; Ernst & Chrobot-Mason, 2011; Gren et al., 2015; Harraf et al., 2015; Hess, 2014; Holsapple & Li, 2008; Schwandt, 1995; Teece et al., 2016; Worley et al., 2014

Decision-Making Practices	
Decisions are made collaboratively based on expertise rather than on formal authority. Decisions are made by individuals with the most knowledge about the factors surrounding the decision and at the lowest level possible. Decision-makers gather information from both inside and outside the organization (e.g., experts in other parts of the organization and experts outside the organization).	Aghina et al., 2015; Alavi et al., 2014; Breu et al., 2002; Butler & Surace, 2015; Dyer & Shafer, 2003; Gren et al., 2015; Harraf et al., 2015; Jaaron & Backhouse, 2014; Lewis et al., 2015; McGuire & Palus, 2019; Nijssen & Paauwe, 2012

Figure A.4: *Agility Levers*

Leader Actions	
Those in a position of formal authority provide direction (including interpretation of the mission and values) and guidance. Leader behaviors include providing context to members to help frame environmental changes as learning opportunities, encouraging and accepting decisions made by members who have the most expertise and knowledge of a given issue, supporting information sharing, setting mission-aligned goals, managing the culture and values, removing obstacles so that members can focus on goals, and creating a climate of psychological safety and trust. Supervision is based on a coaching and development style.	Aghina et al., 2015; Alavi et al., 2014; Bonilla, 2015; de Oliveira et al., 2012; Doz & Kosonen, 2010; Dyer & Shafer, 2003; Edmondson, 1999, 2012; Gren et al., 2015; Harraf et al., 2015; Hess, 2014; Holbeche, 2015; Hopkin, 2015; Kirkpatrick, 2016; Lewis et al., 2015; Moynihan, 2012; Nijssen & Paauwe, 2012; Pasmore, 2015

Processes	
Some processes are clearly defined and stable, while others are intentionally flexible. The knowledge gained from rapid experiments and pilots is integrated into processes. To adopt changes to processes quickly, contingency plans are created, resources are redeployed as needed, and sufficient capacity and resources exist. Technology is used strategically to quickly improve or replace processes.	Aghina et al., 2015; Bonilla, 2015; Breu et al., 2002; Chung et al., 2014; de Oliveira et al., 2012; Doz & Kosonen, 2010; Dyer & Ericksen, 2006; Dyer & Shafer, 2003; Harraf et al., 2015; Holsapple & Li, 2008; Hopkin, 2015; Lewis et al., 2015; Mahmoudi, 2015; Sambamurthy et al., 2003; Sutcliffe et al., 1999; Teece et al., 2016

Roles	
Some roles are clearly defined, while others are intentionally flexible to allow for rapid experimentation and pilots. Employees are provided with resources to engage in training and development so that they can gain skills before they are needed. Employees possess a range of skills that allow them to be redeployed quickly.	Aghina et al., 2015; Alavi et al., 2014; Boin & van Eeten, 2013; Breu et al., 2002; Butler & Surace, 2015; de Oliveira et al., 2012; Edmondson, 2012; Gren et al., 2015; Holsapple & Li, 2008; Nijssen & Paauwe, 2012

Norms and Expectations	
Employees are expected to share information widely, make decisions based on expertise instead of authority, value diverse perspectives, encourage dissenting views during discussion, value mistakes as learning opportunities, and listen to and respect others' ideas. Employee development is viewed as an investment.	Aghina et al., 2015; Argyris & Schon, 1996; Bonilla, 2015; Edmondson, 1999; Ferreira et al., 2015; Gren et al., 2015; Hess, 2014; Holbeche, 2015; Holsapple & Li, 2008; Hopkin, 2015; Jones et al., 2005; Martin, 2019; Schwandt, 1995; Weick & Sutcliffe, 2015; Worley et al., 2014

Figure A.4: *(continued)*

Organizational Effectiveness	
The organization accomplishes its mission-aligned goals in an effective and timely manner.	Corporate Executive Board, 2014; de Oliveira et al., 2012; Doz & Kosonen, 2010; Edmondson, 1999, 2012; Felipe et al., 2016; Harraf et al., 2015; Holbeche, 2015; Holsapple & Li, 2008; Jaaron & Backhouse, 2014; Sharifi & Zhang, 1999; Worley et al., 2014
Customer Satisfaction	
Customers express satisfaction with the organization's products or services.	Holsapple & Li, 2008
Role Clarity	
Employees understand their job and tasks and how they align with the mission.	Edmondson, 1999, 2012; Holbeche, 2015
Job Satisfaction	
Employees like their work.	Alavi et al., 2014; Edmondson, 1999, 2012; Harraf et al., 2015; Holbeche, 2015
Engagement	
Employees have a sense of purpose and dedication to their work.	Edmondson, 1999, 2012; Hess, 2014; Holbeche, 2015; Jaaron & Backhouse, 2014
Intent to Stay	
Employees intend to remain with the organization for the foreseeable future.	Dyer & Shafer, 2003; Hess, 2014; Holbeche, 2015

Figure A.5: *Outcomes*

OUTCOMES

We identified two types of outcomes that can be used to monitor an organization's progress as it works to enhance its organizational agility (see Figure A.5). First, organization-level outcomes include organizational effectiveness and customer satisfaction. Second, individual-level outcomes include role clarity, job satisfaction, engagement, and intent to stay with the organization.

THE GOVERNMENT ORGANIZATIONAL AGILITY ASSESSMENT

Using the organizational agility framework, we created an evaluative tool to measure an organization's current levels of organizational agility, which we called the Government Organizational Agility Assessment (GOAA).[1] For each variable in the framework, we wrote a series of questions that employees could answer as a way to provide feedback on the organization's current levels of agility.

When we use the GOAA with a group—which might be a branch, division, or department within a larger organization—we usually ask everyone to respond to the questions using an online survey. We then aggregate the responses and gather everyone together to review the results. If we have a large enough group, we often break people into smaller groups to review the results and decide what to do about them. Then we have each small group report on their findings so that everyone can see all of the action items and suggestions.

We use this hands-on format to try to reinforce some of the agility principles: usually the leader of the group does not get a special sneak preview of the results! The leader is usually amenable to this, as it sends the message that everyone is equal when they all see the results at the same time. This format also encourages collaboration. We have witnessed many productive conversations during which hierarchy matters little, as insights are shared by leaders at all levels of the organization, including individual contributors. We find that once people come to a shared understanding of the results, they have spontaneous discussions about what they can to do shift the levers and enhance organizational agility. The action items that they propose usually include ways that they can behave differently to support others as they carry out the routines and ways that they can enhance the routines and shift the levers toward agility.

Of course, there is no magic bullet for transforming an organization. A single assessment like the GOAA is, by itself, not likely to radically change the organization. Everyone in the organization must commit to trying out some new behaviors. Leaders must start things

---

1. Kirkpatrick et al. provides reliability and validity evidence for the GOAA.

rolling by experimenting with their own actions. And they must stick with them, even if they feel uncomfortable at first! Real change will come from not giving up and reverting to traditional organizational principles. It takes time, but in the end it will yield the outcomes that the organization needs to fare well in today's times.

References

Aghina, W., De Smet, A., Murarka, M., & Collins, L. (2015). The keys to organizational agility. *McKinsey Quarterly*, December, 1–5.

Alavi, S., Abd. Wahab, D., Muhamad, N., & Arbab Shirani, B. (2014). Organic structure and organizational learning as the main antecedents of workforce agility. *International Journal of Production Research, 52(21)*, 6273–6295.

Argyris, C., & Schon, D. A. (1996). *Organizational learning II: Theory, method, and practice*. Reading, MA: Addison-Wesley.

Barbaroux, P. (2011). A design-oriented approach to organizational change: Insights from a military case study. *Journal of Organizational Change Management, 24(5)*, 626–639.

Boin, A., & van Eeten, M. J. G. (2013). The resilient organization: A critical appraisal. *Public Management Review, 15(3)*, 429–445.

Bonilla, M. (2015). Building resilience in small nonprofits. *OD Practitioner, 47(1)*, 8–14.

Breu, K., Hemingway, S. J., Strathern, M., & Bridger, D. (2002). Workforce agility: The new employee strategy for the knowledge economy. *Journal of Information Technology, 17(1)*, 21–31.

Brueller, N. N., Carmeli, A., & Drori, I. (2014). How do different types of mergers and acquisitions facilitate strategic agility? *California Management Review, 56(3)*, 39–57.

Butler, B., & Surace, K. (2015). Call for organizational agility in the emergent sector of the service industry. *Journal of Business Management, 10*, 4–14.

Cegarra-Navarro, J., Soto-Acosta, P., & Wensley, A. K. P. (2016). Structured knowledge processes and firm performance: The role of organizational agility. *Journal of Business Research, 69*, 1544–1549.

Chung, S., Lee, K. Y., & Kim, K. (2014). Job performance through mobile enterprise systems: The role of organizational agility, location independence, and task characteristics. *Information & Management, 51*, 605–617.

Corporate Executive Board. (2014). *Driving workforce agility in the public sector: Agile strategies for an uncertain environment*. Washington, DC: Corporate Executive Board.

Davenport, T. H., & Prusak, L. (2000). *Working knowledge: How organizations manage what they know*. Boston, MA: Harvard Business School Press.

De Florio, V. (2014). Quality indicators for collective systems resilience. *Emergence: Complexity & Organization, 16(3)*, 65–104.

de Oliveira, M. A., Valentina, L. V. O. D., & Possamai, O. (2012). Forecasting project performance considering the influence of leadership style on organizational agility. *International Journal of Productivity & Performance Management, 61(6)*, 653–671.

Doz, Y. L., & Kosonen, M. (2010). Embedding strategic agility: A leadership agenda for accelerating business model renewal. *Long Range Planning, 43(2–3)*, 370–382.

Dyer, L., & Ericksen, J. (2006). *Dynamic organizations: Achieving marketplace agility through human resource scalability*. (CAHRS working paper). Ithaca, NY: Cornell University.

Dyer, L., & Shafer, R. A. (2003). Dynamic organizations: Achieving marketplace and organizational agility with people. (CAHRS working paper). Ithaca, NY: Cornell University.

Edmondson, A. (1999). Psychological safety and learning behavior in work teams. *Administrative Science Quarterly, 44*, 350–383.

Edmondson, A. (2012). *Teaming: How organizations learn, innovate, and compete in the knowledge economy.* San Francisco, CA: Jossey-Bass.

Ernst, C., & Chrobot-Mason, D. (2011). *Boundary spanning leadership: Six practices for solving problems, driving innovation, and transforming organizations.* New York, NY: McGraw-Hill.

Felipe, C. M., Roldán, J. L., & Leal-Rodríguez, A. L. (2016). An explanatory and predictive model for organizational agility. *Journal of Business Research, 69(10)*, 4624–4631.

Ferreira, J. J. M., Fernandes, C., Alves, H., & Raposo, M. L. (2015). Drivers of innovation strategies: Testing the Tidd and Bessant (2009) model. *Journal of Business Research, 68(7)*, 1395–1403.

Fleming, R. S. (2012). Ensuring organizational resilience in times of crisis. *Journal of Global Business Issues, 6(1)*, 31–34.

Galbraith, J. R. (2014). *Designing organizations: Strategy, structure, and process at the business unit and enterprise levels.* San Francisco: Jossey-Bass.

Gren, L., Torkar, R., & Feldt, R. (2015). The prospects of a quantitative measurement of agility: A validation study on an agile maturity model. *The Journal of Systems and Software, 107*, 38–49.

Hamel, G., & Välikangas, L. (2003). The quest for resilience. *Harvard Business Review*, September, 52–63.

Harraf, A., Wanasika, I., Tate, K., & Talbott, K. (2015). Organizational agility. *Journal of Applied Business Research, 31(2)*, 675–686.

Hess, E. D. (2014). *Learn or die: Using science to build a leading-edge learning organization.* New York, NY: Columbia Business School Publishing.

Holbeche, L. (2015). *The agile organization: How to build an innovative, sustainable and resilient business.* London: KoganPage.

Holsapple, C. W., & Li, X. (2008). Understanding organizational agility: A work-design perspective. *Proceedings of the International Command and Control Research and Technology Symposium, 937*, 1–25.

Hopkin, P. (2015). Achieving enhanced organizational resilience by improved management of risk: Summary of research into the principles of resilience and the practices of resilient organisations. *Journal of Business Continuity & Emergency Planning, 8(3)*, 252–262.

Jaaron, A. A. M., & Backhouse, C. J. (2014). Service organisations resilience through the application of the vanguard method of systems thinking: A case study approach. *International Journal of Production Research, 52(7)*, 2026–2041.

Jones, R. A., Jimmieson, N. L., & Griffiths, A. (2005). The impact of organizational culture and reshaping capabilities on change implementation success: The mediating role of readiness for change. *Journal of Management Studies, 42(2)*, 361–386.

Kirkpatrick, S. A. (2016). *Build a better vision statement: Extending research with practical advice.* Lanham, MD: Lexington Books.

Kirkpatrick, S. A., Miller, S. C., Terragnoli, A., & Sprenger, A. (In press). Development of an organizational agility assessment for government and nonprofit organizations. *Organization Development Journal.*

Lewis, M. W., Andriopoulos, C., & Smith, W. K. (2015). Paradoxical leadership to enable strategic agility. *California Management Review, 56(3)*, 58–77.

Mahmoudi, O. (2015). The impact of e-government on organizational agility: Case study of governmental banks in Iran. *International Journal of Management, 2(10)*, 1141–1160.

Martin, S. (Ed.). (2019). *Feedback that works* (2nd edition). Greensboro, NC: Center for Creative Leadership Press.

McGuire, J., & Palus, C. (2019). *Vertical development: Culture still wins over strategy* [White paper]. Retrieved January 21, 2021, from the Center for Creative Leadership website (ccl.org): vertical-leadership-development-for-executive-teams-culture-wins-over-strategy.pdf

Moynihan, D. P. (2012). A theory of culture-switching: Leadership and red-tape during Hurricane Katrina. *Public Administration, 90(4)*, 851–868.

Nejatian, M., & Zarei, M. H. (2013). Moving towards organizational agility: Are we improving in the right direction? *Global Journal of Flexible Systems Management, 14(4)*, 241–253.

Nijssen, M., & Paauwe, J. (2012). HRM in turbulent times: How to achieve organizational agility? *International Journal of Human Resource Management, 23(16)*, 3315–3335.

O'Reilly, C. A., & Tushman, M. L. (2004). The ambidextrous organization. *Harvard Business Review*, April, 74–81.

Orton, J. D., & Weick, K. E. (1990). Loosely coupled systems: A reconceptualization. *Academy of Management Review, 15(2)*, 203–223.

Overby, E., Bharadwaj, A., & Sambamurthy, V. (2006). Enterprise agility and the enabling role of information technology. *European Journal of Information Systems, 15*, 120–131.

Pasmore, W. (2015). *Leading continuous change: Navigating churn in the real world.* Oakland, CA: Berrett-Koehler.

Pellissier, R. (2012). A proposed frame of reference for complexity management as opposed to the established linear management strategies. *International Journal of Organizational Innovation, 5(2)*, 6–67.

Sambamurthy, V., Bharadwaj, A., & Grover, V. (2003). Shaping agility through digital options: Reconceptualizing the role of information technology in contemporary firms. *MIS Quarterly, 27(2)*, 237–263.

Schwandt, D. R. (1995). Learning as an organization: A journey in chaos. In S. Chawla & J. Renesch (Eds.), *Learning organizations: Developing cultures for tomorrow's workplace* (pp. 365–380). San Francisco, CA: New Leaders Press.

Sharifi, H., & Zhang, Z. (1999). A methodology for achieving agility in manufacturing organisations: An introduction. *International Journal of Production Economics, 20(4)*, 496–512.

Sutcliffe, K., Sitkin, S., & Browning, L. (1999). Tailoring process management to situational requirements. In R. Cole & W. Scott (Eds.), *The quality movement and organization theory* (pp. 315–330). Thousand Oaks, CA: Sage.

Teece, D., Peteraf, M., & Leih, S. (2016). Dynamic capabilities and organizational agility: Risk, uncertainty, and strategy in the innovation economy. *California Management Review, 58(4)*, 13–36.

Weick, K. E., & Sutcliffe, K. M. (2015). *Managing the unexpected: Sustained performance in a complex world* (3rd edition). Hoboken, NJ: Wiley.

Worley, C. G., Williams, T., & Lawler, E. E. (2014). *The agility factor: Building adaptable organizations for superior performance.* San Francisco, CA: Jossey-Bass.

Zhang, D. Z. (2011). Towards theory building in agile manufacturing strategies—Case studies of an agility taxonomy. *International Journal of Production Economics, 131(1)*, 303–331.

Acknowledgments

We could not have written this book without considerable help from many people. We appreciate the support and encouragement that Elaine Ward and Nancy Letsinger have given us over the past several years as our agility work has evolved and grown. We owe our start to this work to our cherished colleague Suzanne Geigle, who always has new insights and ideas to share with us. We sincerely thank Sanith Wijesinghe for supporting our research. We appreciate the funding that our work has received as part of the MITRE Innovation Program. We deeply appreciate our coauthors and colleagues—Jennifer Myers, Jamie Ann Neidig, Awais Sheikh, Jessica Tierney, and Greg Waldrip—whose deep expertise greatly improved the chapters they contributed to. We received considerable help from Khudadad Cheema, who read drafts with fresh eyes and told us where we had disconnects or incomplete ideas and needed more relevant examples. We cannot begin to convey how grateful we are for Marilyn Kupetz and her superb editing skills; she was also instrumental in helping us conceptualize the book, which made it more engaging and readable. We are also indebted to the reviewers—Peter Baverso, Sarah Modlin, and Jim Wylde—for their constructive advice that improved the book. And our editor Charlotte Ashlock was a pleasure to work with, as were Kate Gibson and Lynn Everett. We pass along our thanks to them and everyone at Berrett-Koehler for their support.

Index

Note: Information in figures is indicated by *f*.

About the Authors

Sarah Miller is an organization development consultant at The MITRE Corporation, a not-for-profit organization that operates research and development centers for the federal government. She has worked with individuals and groups in the corporate, education, government, and non-profit sectors internationally through coaching, leadership development, and organizational effectiveness initiatives. Prior to MITRE, Sarah worked at the Center for Creative Leadership, Red Hat, and in her own consulting practice. Sarah holds an MA from the University of Michigan at Ann Arbor and a BA from the University of North Carolina at Chapel Hill. She earned a certificate in Organizational Development from Columbia University.

Shelley Kirkpatrick, PhD, is a principal at The MITRE Corporation, a not-for-profit organization that operates research and development centers for the federal government. She is also an adjunct professor of human resource management at George Mason University. A former professor at Carnegie Mellon University and the American University, Shelley has authored more than fifty publications on company vision statements, leadership, motivation, training evaluation, and workforce assessment. As founder of Visiontelligence, LLC, she applies her research on company vision statements to help entrepreneurs grow their business. She is the author of *Build a Better Vision Statement*. She earned her PhD from the University of Maryland at College Park and her BS from Bowling Green State University.

About the Contributors

Jennifer Myers is a principal at The MITRE Corporation, a not-for-profit organization that operates research and development centers for the federal government. As a behavioral scientist and advisor to federal government leaders, she guides agencies to develop human performance strategies that drive transformational change and organizational improvement. Jennifer is actively involved in public-sector human capital forums, including the American Council for Technology-Industry Advisory Council (ACT-IAC) Talent as a Service (TaaS) series. She maintains strategic human-capital certifications from the Human Resource Certification Institute (HRCI SPHR) and the Society for Human Resource Management (SHRM-SCP). Jennifer earned her BS from Miami University (Ohio) and her MBA from the University of Maryland at College Park.

Jamie Ann Neidig is a principal at The MITRE Corporation, a not-for-profit organization that operates research and development centers for the federal government. Jamie's expertise is in strategic planning and human-capital management. She has taught human resource management at George Mason University and served as a guest lecturer at James Madison University. She earned her MBA from the Tuck School of Business at Dartmouth College and a BA from Cornell University as well as certificates from New York University and the Massachusetts Institute of Technology.

Awais Sheikh is a strategic planning and innovation expert for the Amazon Web Services (AWS) federal and nonprofit vertical. He was formerly the business innovation capability lead at The MITRE Corporation, a not-for-profit organization that operates research and development centers for the federal government. He has expertise in design thinking and lean startup to help organizations explore complex problem areas and generate solution concepts to be tested. Awais's research on innovation and design thinking has appeared in the *Journal for Public Performance Management Review* and the *Defense Acquisition Research Journal*. He earned a BS and an MBA from Virginia Tech, and he is pursuing a master's degree in innovation management and entrepreneurship from Temple University.

Jessica Tierney is a business-process improvement expert at The MITRE Corporation, a not-for-profit organization that operates research and development centers for the federal government. Her work focuses on applying multidisciplinary systems-engineering and business-process transformation approaches. Jessica also leads the Business Process Management Community of Practice at MITRE. She is a certified Lean Six Sigma black belt and certified by the Object Management Group® in business process management. Jessica earned a BA from Marymount University and is pursuing a master's degree in systems engineering leadership from Worcester Polytechnic Institute.

Greg Waldrip is a business strategist at The MITRE Corporation, a not-for-profit organization that operates research and development centers for the federal government. Before joining MITRE, he led pollution prevention and industry partnership programs at several federal government agencies. He holds a BS in biology and an MS in environmental science from Yale University.

Berrett–Koehler
Publishers

Berrett-Koehler is an independent publisher dedicated to an ambitious mission: *Connecting people and ideas to create a world that works for all.*

Our publications span many formats, including print, digital, audio, and video. We also offer online resources, training, and gatherings. And we will continue expanding our products and services to advance our mission.

We believe that the solutions to the world's problems will come from all of us, working at all levels: in our society, in our organizations, and in our own lives. Our publications and resources offer pathways to creating a more just, equitable, and sustainable society. They help people make their organizations more humane, democratic, diverse, and effective (and we don't think there's any contradiction there). And they guide people in creating positive change in their own lives and aligning their personal practices with their aspirations for a better world.

And we strive to practice what we preach through what we call "The BK Way." At the core of this approach is *stewardship,* a deep sense of responsibility to administer the company for the benefit of all of our stakeholder groups, including authors, customers, employees, investors, service providers, sales partners, and the communities and environment around us. Everything we do is built around stewardship and our other core values of *quality, partnership, inclusion,* and *sustainability.*

This is why Berrett-Koehler is the first book publishing company to be both a B Corporation (a rigorous certification) and a benefit corporation (a for-profit legal status), which together require us to adhere to the highest standards for corporate, social, and environmental performance. And it is why we have instituted many pioneering practices (which you can learn about at www.bkconnection.com), including the Berrett-Koehler Constitution, the Bill of Rights and Responsibilities for BK Authors, and our unique Author Days.

We are grateful to our readers, authors, and other friends who are supporting our mission. We ask you to share with us examples of how BK publications and resources are making a difference in your lives, organizations, and communities at www.bkconnection.com/impact.

Dear reader,

Thank you for picking up this book and welcome to the worldwide BK community! You're joining a special group of people who have come together to create positive change in their lives, organizations, and communities.

What's BK all about?

Our mission is to connect people and ideas to create a world that works for all.

Why? Our communities, organizations, and lives get bogged down by old paradigms of self-interest, exclusion, hierarchy, and privilege. But we believe that can change. That's why we seek the leading experts on these challenges—and share their actionable ideas with you.

A welcome gift

To help you get started, we'd like to offer you a **free copy** of one of our bestselling ebooks:

www.bkconnection.com/welcome

When you claim your **free ebook**, you'll also be subscribed to our blog.

Our freshest insights

Access the best new tools and ideas for leaders at all levels on our blog at ideas.bkconnection.com.

Sincerely,

Your friends at Berrett-Koehler

Certified

Corporation